The Spirit of
Warriors

Conceived in South Sudan,
Born in Ugandan, Discovered in America

Lilian Okech

Manufactured in the United States of America

ISBN: 979-8-9861473-9-0

Library of Congress Control Number: 2022923859

Follow Lilian Okech

Social Media Outlets:
Facebook: www.facebook.com/LilianOkech89
Instagram: @lilianokech
Email: lilian@lilianokech.com
Website: www.lilianokech.com

CONTENTS

Acknowledgements. i

Dedication. iii

Introduction. v

The History of Us; Who Are The Luo/Acholi People?. 1

Our Life Before War 3

Our Power and Community; What Makes Us Different 5

Unity and Love; Our Roots for One Another. 7

Going Back Home. 17

Living As A Refugee. 25

Coming To America. 29

Starting High School 37

Pregnant At Sixteen 41

Kicked Out of the House 45

Forced Into Marriage 47

My First Child 51

I Knew It Was Not Going To Work 57

My Daughter 61

Pregnant Again 85

Moving To Iowa 87

Healing 89

Getting Off Of Housing Assistance .93

Habitat 97

Baptism 99

Development Class 103

My Spirit Troubled Me 105

Jail 109

My Love 119

Fasting 125

Whatever You Lock on Earth will be Locked in Heaven 129

Transformation 137

Management 139

Queen 143

Acknowledgements

To my creator, thank you for protecting me when I was in my mother's womb. As we fled from South Sudan to Uganda, your eye was on us. You saved me from cancer when I was one year old and brought me back to life when I was nine.

To my strong and wonderful mother, Aurelia Ayot Nathaniel, thank you for your sacrifices as a single mother to care for your eight children; your hard work will not be forgotten. You put school first and you made sure we all went to school. Whether you were cutting a tree, making a shackle, or working in a garden all day long, you reminded us that if we could work hard, we would never go hungry. Because of you, we will pass on our hard work ethic to our children and let them know that hard work guarantees success in the future. Mom, I just want to say thank you for everything you have done in our lives; forever you will be in my heart.

To Langoya James Arop, I am forever grateful to you for always being with me. We made a promise under a mango tree fifteen years ago. Thank you for standing beside me and being my advisor, brother, counselor, and best friend.

To my boys, Mama loves you all very much. Thank you for keeping me going in life. I hope I have shown you that with hard work, success is possible.

To my family and friends, thank you for your support and love.

To Dr. Denise Nicholson and Les Brown, I could not be the woman I am today without your help. I am forever grateful for your belief in me; thank you.

To my struggles and pain, thank you for giving birth to purpose and teaching me lessons for a lifetime.

To all the powerful women in our history, thank you for paving the way for us. The path you prepared through your tears and sacrifices opened the door to a world of opportunities.

Dedication

I dedicate this book to my Beloved Father God, who has chosen me among millions to present as an ambassador in his Kingdom. By your words I stand.

To all refugees and immigrants worldwide who lost their families, home, and country due to conflicts, I pray you find your voice and build your confidence to keep going. I understand it's hard, but you have come too far to quit now.

To all of the girls who've been forced into marriage, you're not alone. I hope you find yourself and the strength to become the person you are meant to be.

To all women who got pregnant unexpectedly and found themselves in a relationship that wasn't meant to be, yet you still found a way to make the world a better place, I hope you find peace within your heart.

To all of the mothers who fight on their knees to make sure their children grow up right, God is with you.

To my mother, the one who never went to school, but knew how important education was for her children. She worked hard day and night, ensuring we all got an education. Without her dedication to our lives, there would be no Lilian. Thank you, I love you so much, Mom.

To all dynamic women who don't care about what the world says about them. They stand up and demand their rights, demand their position, and carry it with pride, keep it up Queens!

To all of the powerful women in my life whose names might not be known, but without whom I would not have finished this book.

Nina Loan, my English Second Language (ESL) teacher, who began teaching me my ABCs in the ninth grade, your patience and love for refugees in America will never be forgotten. I love you and thank you for everything you have done in my life.

Introduction

Why is it that when it comes to power, everyone and everything wants to be powerful? But how does it feel when your power and everything you knew and love, has been taken away from you in the blink of an eye? When you wake up in smoke and unbelievable noise, in that instant, your life changes forever. You wake up in terror. All you hear is crying, born of deep anguish that shocks your brain like electricity. You forget to breathe, your blood stops flowing and your heart cries out for help.

These are indescribable moments that can never be fully expressed for the world to understand. That is the life of over 80 million immigrants in the world today. My mind always goes back to the shock I felt when I was first asked, "Where do you come from? Why are you here? What made you come to this country? Do you like it here?" My brain races back to the past; *How can I answer these questions? Do I not belong here? Should I have been asking the same questions when people arrived in my country?* I do not remember asking anyone these questions. We welcomed people with love, and we honored them with authority.

We put everything we were doing aside to give our time to them. We made sure they were well taken care of. We did not show weakness. We do right to mankind. But we didn't know that those actions were not universal. The niceties and kindness we offered were used against us.

That is the story for Africans and many other immigrants throughout the world. This book reflects the experience of many people who lost their homes and everything they had to start a new life; after facing struggles that are unspeakable to many today.

In the society we live in today, everyone wants to do something good, but some don't know how. That is why your silence will not serve the world. Whether we are posting pictures on social media or going Live in the world of social media, let it be to the benefit of humankind. Whatever we do as human beings, whether good or bad, is because our spirit is crying out for a better life, and we are created to dominate our environment.

Genesis 1:26 (NKJV) says, "Then God said, let us make man in our image, according to our likeness; let them have dominion over the fish of the sea, and over the birds of the air, and over the cattle, over all the earth and over every creeping thing that creeps on the earth." I strongly believe that I was born to do something great, and it doesn't depend on my location.

I know America has played a big role in my life. I have gained the knowledge and wisdom to create a new life for myself and my family. There are some people, however, whose lives and families have been destroyed in America. It all comes down to our mindset. What you choose to see determines your reality. You have the power to change your reality by shifting your focus and believing in what you want to see in your future. "For as he thinks in his heart, so is he" (Proverbs 23: 7 NKJV). I chose to think positively. I chose to change my thinking to make a difference in the world. I chose to be me. I hope you will choose to join millions who decide not to let their circumstances determine their future.

Genesis 26:3

"Stay in this area land for a while, and I will be with you and will bless you. For to you and your descendants, I will give all these lands and confirm the oath I swore to your father, Abraham. But what will you do now, if you are no longer in your father's land, the lands that been promised to you?"

The History of Us;
Who Are The Luo/Acholi People?

Early in 1989, in Northern Uganda, East Africa, I was born to Morris Okech Adala, my father, and Auerlia Ayot Nathanial, my mother. My grandfather, Nathanial, was a son of Pollo, Pollo was the son of Modi, Modi was the son of Oyenga, Oyenga, was the son of Opiyo, Opiyo, immigrated from Lokoro, (Pari) in South Sudan to Pajok South Sudan. My father is the son of Vinansio Adala, my grandfather, from Panyikwar, South Sudan. Our history is that we are the Nilotic ethnic group that inhabits an area ranging from Egypt, Sudan, and Ethiopia, through Northern Uganda and eastern Congo (DRC), into Western Kenya, and the Mara Region of Tanzania.

The Luo language belongs to the Western branch of the Nilotic family. The group in South Sudan included the Shilluk, Anuak, Pari, Balanda Boor, Thuri, Luwo and Acholi (that is my people). The Acholi people (also spelled Acoli) are a Luo nation found in Magwi County, in South Sudan and Northern Uganda (an area commonly referred to as Acholi land). This includes the districts of Agago, Amuru, Gulu, Nwoya, Pader, Lamow, and Kitgum. That is where I was born. When my family fled from South Sudan, we left our home because of the war from 1988-1989. My mother was pregnant with me and soon when we arrived at the first camp in Uganda, I entered the world. I don't know my real birthday, because my mom doesn't remember. I do not have a birth certificate because it was lost when our house caught on fire.

My mom said I was born around November or March. I chose November, because a lot of good things happened to me in November. This is common in our community, we call it Sudanese birthdays. My documents say I was born on January 1st. People would always say, "You're a New Years' baby," and this was a surprise to me too.

In August 2021, I had the opportunity to take a journey throughout the Acholi land, and it was one of the most beautiful moments, and one I will cherish for the rest of my life. I was born in Northern Uganda, the United Nations moved us to a different camp called Kiryandongo. I haven't been North, but there is something beautiful about knowing where you come from. When we were driving through Northern Uganda going to South Sudan, there was a feeling of peace in my heart. Going from Bweyale to Kitgum, our car broke down right after we crossed Lake Karuma, but there was no fear.

My mind had to get used to everyone speaking a language I understood. This gave me an indescribable feeling of gratitude for my native tongue. Our driver just ran back across the bridge and got help. Everyone was there for each other, looking at the guardsman who guarded the National park. We stayed there for about two hours and it was all worth it. Since I was young, I had heard about the Karuma Bridge. People have lost their lives there, but there I was looking at it in awe. It was a very powerful lake. I heard the water roaring strong, and up the hill, the Chinese began building an energy line to help Northern Uganda. These were good things.. I was happy, I was home. My journey to South Sudan was more difficult. I never thought I would make it to my mother's village.

The Spirit of Warriors: Remember your roots, when you know it.

CHAPTER TWO

Our Life Before War

When my great-great maternal grandfather immigrated from Lokoro to a village called Pajok, there were already some tribes living there, but they didn't know. My people arrived in the area around early 1600, the name Pajok came when they arrived in the village. They didn't see anyone, but there was water and good land. The leader called Rowt/ Ruel (meaning King) said let us immigrate here and call it our home.

They started settling, and when some of the members stepped out to collect water, on their way back, they came across a fully prepared meal ready for them! There were all kinds of foods there: dried meat cooked with peanut butter, and other greens like osuga, malagwand, oyadoo, akuura, aloot, poow, lakotokoto (the stews cooked with raw sesame), and kwon (a millet flour mix in hot water). They were surprised, and they went back to where they were staying. They told the leader that they found food and no one was there to claim it, and their leader said it was okay for them to eat it. After eating, they decided as a group to stay there.

They decided to start a new name for the people, so they came up with Pajok, meaning the spirit. They believed the spirit fed them, and there was one man in the group who did not grab any food when people were eating. He thought they were going to hand food to people, and when everyone finished eating, he went to Rowt and told Rowt that he and his family didn't eat. He said, "I thought they were going to hand it out." They asked if he hadn't seen people eating and told him that if he wanted to be stupid, he could die of hunger. Because of him, his family name was Obwolto (meaning the stupid one die).

This is the name of my mom's family from the clan of Pajok. There are seven clans in Acholi of South Sudan. My Father is Acholi from panyikwara (Iwire) and we also have Palwar, Magwi, Omeo, Agoro and Obbo where my grandmother is from. I do not know the meaning of other clans, but I know our people. There is always a reason behind a name. After settling and getting to know the place, they found out there were people there, and they had a King too.

The people of Pajok took territory and power away from the King, and put him in jail. Not house jail; back then, there was no such thing. The purpose was to remove his power so he could no longer rule. The Pajok King took power and rule over all of the people there. As they settled, every family started to build their hut, and they structured it with a round roof and square base, with the compound in the middle for the kids to play. There was storytelling in the evening around the fireplace.

Back then, we did not have a notebook or pen to write our stories. Our history went from generation to generation from seeing the work and hearing stories around the fireplace.

In the mornings, the boys went with their father to the forest to collect the finest wood to build the hut; or they'd go to the garden to plant food, while women woke up early in the morning to go collect water with their young girls. As we grew up doing things with our parents, lessons were passed on, to the next generation.

The Spirit of Warriors: Get all the knowledge you can from your community and continue to keep it alive.

CHAPTER THREE

Our Power and Community; What Makes Us Different

My maternal grandfather was born around 1920, in the village of Pajok (Obwolto). When a baby is born, if it is a boy, the mother and the baby stay inside for three days. The elders get a local rod and tie it around the compound of the home so that no one other than close family members could enter for three days. If a baby girl is born, they do the same thing for four days. After three or four days, the family comes together, as the elders point out the "good-looking" chicken for the celebration.

Young boys catch the chicken, and the women of the village start preparing for the occasion by getting grain and pounding grain in their mortars for food. They prepare traditional foods cooked in earthen pots over a fire built among three rocks. The food is dried meat hunted from the forests and cooked with peanut butter, black-eyed beans, with the skin off cooked in porridge, and shea butter oil on top. The chicken is for the umbilical cord. They will kill the chicken at the place where they buried the placenta for the blood to drip over the place. When the chicken is cooked only elders can eat it. Before the chicken is killed, one of the older elders takes the chicken around over the child. If it is a boy, the chicken is taken around three times, and if it is a girl, four times. This is done to cast out any bad sprits, and welcome the baby into the family.

Young girls are to help with collecting water as the women cook and others are preparing local wine the night before the celebration. When everything is prepared, it's time to name the baby. Most of our names meant something. As they eat and drink into the evening, they finish the celebration with dancing to the drum. After the celebration, the mother goes to the river to collect water as others see her. They show her respect by letting her get her water first, because she has a newborn baby at home. The community continues to care for her, for two weeks after she gives birth so she can heal.

There is no pain medication for new mothers to alleviate the pain. The elder mothers were taught by their mothers to take care of the mother. They bathe her in extremely hot water to release any clotted blood. Some women die after birth, because they are afraid of the hot water. Most of the time, they force the mother into the hot water to prevent blood clotting. Sometimes they hold her down, so they can save her life. It isn't done to hurt the women, that is how they can get healing and it has been done from generation to generation.

The Spirit of Warriors: Don't take life for granted

CHAPTER FOUR

Unity and Love; Our Roots for One Another

They celebrate the young baby and bless him to prosper in his time. Back then, we did not know about Christianity or any other religion, but believed in the spirit that protects us from evil doing. Then, they also had a King who controlled the rain. If there was any sickness in the village, they sacrificed a Goat, lamb, or chicken to their gods to cast out any bad spirits that came upon them.

The King of the rain was given by nature to the chosen one. As you walked on the street, you could find two rocks moving. When you notice the rock and you can get it, and bring it home, you put it in a bowl made from pumpkin. The pumpkin was cut in half, and all the insides are taken out while the skin is left to dry. Then you scrub the inside to make it smooth for use. Some use it for carrying water, others use it to eat from, like a plate. Back then we didn't have things like cookware or silverware. Everything was made out of God's created nation.

Keeping the rock in your hut allowed you to control the rain. If it was the season for planning and it was dry, everyone in your clan helped you with something small to bless the land with rain. As soon as you put water in the bowl with the rock, it starts raining right away. They asked in peace because they knew that he was chosen to protect the village. Even though they didn't know anything about God or the Bible, their life was at peace, they followed leaders as they live, and there was no hospital, if anyone got sick. They depended on natural remedies and ingredients to get well. As they settled in their new place, in order to identify safe fruit to eat, they would eat what the birds ate. They decided that if the fruit does not kill the birds, it won't kill humans.

The Acholi people are known to be hard workers. When they settled in the village of Pajok, they started to build huts, cut down the trees, and plant grain and vegetables. They would go as a group to every family garden. It was the men's job to cut down trees and the grass. After the grass is dry. They bound it to clear the way to start digging and planning. Women were to cook for men and do light work, like collecting grass or picking up wood. Everyone worked together and supported each other.

Unity and Love

My grandfather found his way in the world by watching his father and learning from him. My grandfather saw his father doing things around the home: building their hut, fixing arrows and tribe wood for hunting, and telling stories by the fireplace in the evening after dinner. They shared the love of the community! An old African proverb says *it takes a village to raise a child*. My grandfather's dad would go to the garden and his mom would leave home to collect water and cook for her husband. She would take the food to him.

It was tradition for her to cook for her husband and leave some food at home for the kids for lunch. When she would take the food, she also had to pick the weeds in the garden and help clean up after her husband. The kids were left at home with the elders who were no longer able to work hard in the garden. As elders, they cared for all of the children as their own, and curious young boys and girls would always try to do things they saw their parents doing. Kids were trained by elders through the elders telling the stories in parables. This would prepare the children for life. One of the parables stuck with me, and it was about a child who is stubborn and not a good listener to his parents.

My mom would begin as we sat around the fireplace picking up the row of green sesame. It would be ready, but not dry yet, because it would be the season for less food. They pick the green sesame for us to crack it open and put it out in the sun for a day to dry. We cleaned it up and made sesame butter out of it as we sat and listened to mom tell stories that have been passed on from generation to generation.

Here is the story about a boy who was not a good listener:

One day, a mother and her four children finished eating dinner, and they sat around the fire. It was raining, the fire was not burning anymore in their hut, and the father was visiting other villages. A man who was not from their village entered the hut, and the mother knew he was not a good man. She quickly covered up the fires with ashes, and gave the kids a look so that they would know that their life might be in danger and that they should not say anything. The man asked the mother if there was a fire, because he wanted to smoke. She said no, but said she could get it for him, and he agreed. She asked her kids if they could go to the neighbor's house to get fire.

She asked the kids who were willing and who were good listeners. As the kid left, the mother said a secret word, "Manyamalamanyamany," it means don't come back. They waited, and the kid didn't come back, so again, the mother asked one of the other kids to go check on their sister. The mother said she didn't know why the child didn't come back. The second child agreed to go get the sister, and never came back. Again the mother asked the third child, and said, "I am not sure what is going on with these kids, can you go and please tell your brother and sister that the visitor wants to smoke?" That child agreed and he left. The mother again gave the secret word.

The mother knew the last child was stubborn. She asked the fourth child to go check on his brothers and sister, and said that they weren't usually like this. She said if there is no fire, they will come back. The fourth child said, "No, I am not going." So, the mother said she would go check on them, beause she was not sure what was taking them so long. As soon as she left, the fourth child said, "I don't understand my mom. We just finished eating and we have fire here. There you go, you can smoke now." The man said ok, got out the local cigarette which was rolled into paper and ready for smoking, he lit it up and smoked. When he finished, he killed the boy and left the village. The story is to help children to be good kids and listen to their parents.

It was a beautiful day, and all of the children in my neighborhood came together under a big tree, and we were playing and pretending to be husband and wife. Girls are to choose their husbands and take care of the house as good wives should be. We build our homes with sticks and grass, use cans for cooking, and some old clothes for bedding. This was a fun game to prepare young people for their future. I heard my mom calling me from hundreds of feet away from home. I dropped the food I was cooking for my "husband" and I ran towards my mom's voice. When I got closest to her, she stopped me and told me to call my sister Regina. I said okay, and I could hear from her voice, she was crying for help.

I ran as fast as my feet could, with panic, I found my sister, grounding sesame butter to make soup. I told her mom was calling her. It was like my sister knew what was happening. She dropped everything she was doing and ran towards mom. I was behind her. I wondered what it could be. When we got closer, my mom said something, and my sister turned to me and told me to go back home. What? I was more concerned, but in my time as a child, I knew to obey adults and listen without question, so I said, "yes ma'am," and turned around and ran back home.

I couldn't go back and play anymore. I was curious about what was going on. About five minutes later, I saw my sister come home with something wrapped up and making noise. It sounded like a baby, and when she got closer, she called me and said, "Look at your little sister." Wow, mom was having a baby, but why was she left in the garden? My sister saw concern and said mom is fine. She said mom would come home soon, then she put the baby on the bed and went to clean mom up with water.

After the placenta came out, thirty minutes later, I saw mom walking home slowly, and her stomach was smaller. In my mind, I knew she had the baby, but I did not understand how. Women back then didn't know anything about hospitals or family planning (birth control). I began learning about and being taught about how to be a mother at the age of five. We started taking care of babies. They would put the baby on your back with a handmade baby carrier and wrap them with a piece of clothing. There were schools, but people didn't know much about education.

At the age of fourteen, we started to take full responsibility for the house. We walked for a mile to get wood for cooking. It was more like showing off our womanhood. We did it in the Winter when the temperature is really hot. When all of the grass was dry, all of the girls in the neighborhood got together and go to the forest to get some wood. We lined them up around the tree perfectly so that when spring came with rain and planning season, we would have wood for cooking. As a young girl, I really didn't understand this, but I just saw my mother doing it. I was motivated to do it too, so we woke up early in the morning and went together.

Early in the morning, around 6 AM, we walked for about one hour before we got some wood. We brought water and food to eat, such as papaya, mango, corn, and cassava. As we walked for a mile, talking and having fun, we talked about the guys who liked us, what we were learning in school, and what we wanted for Christmas. My best friend, Susan, always talked about how she could take care of her husband's house, and that school meant nothing to her. She was a beautiful, strong woman, she loved to run. I believe she was one of the strongest among us all, she could gather the most wood and carry the most wood, she walked so fast we would have to catch up to her.

We were the same age, but Susan was so mature and knew so much about men, that I was learning from her. She was the first in our group to start getting her period at the age of fourteen. We were all so curious and wanted to know the how, where, and what, because we never talked about getting periods with our mothers. Most of the girls got their periods at the age of sixteen, and it was not considered a good thing to get your period early in age. Girls who did were seen to be bad girls, or they were already used by a man. I wish our parents explained more, but thank goodness in 2004, there were organizations that taught young girls about their body, and gave pads to girls.

When we went to the forest, we decided to collect the wood that some of the guys cut so they could bound it for coals, and then sell it in the local market to make money. On our last day, we chose to get the wood those men cut. My friend Jene told us not to, but we didn't listen and collected the best wood. As we continued getting all the wood, cutting it, and making it into a ship that we can put together and tie with a rope to come home, some of our other friends wisely chose not to touch anybody's stuff. Me, Susan, and one of my other friends got the wood. Two hours later the guys came to check on their wood and found us taking their wood.

As soon as they saw us they slowed down and tried to catch us. I wasn't sure what was on their minds, but I knew whatever it was, it wasn't going to be good! We saw them before they caught us, so we dropped everything and started running. They started running up to us. Thank goodness we were fast. When I looked back, one of the men was only about ten feet away from my best friend Susan. I screamed so loud, and Susan sped up and ran as fast as she could. It felt like it was life or death because we didn't know what they'd do if they caught us. We were running for our lives. We escaped! I don't know how we got away, but we finally found one of the friends who decided not to touch anyone's wood. It was not a fun day any more. We did not get home until 6 PM.

I told my mother what happened and that it would be our last day going to the forest to collect wood. She really didn't say much, because she knew what they used to do so she gave me the time to explore the forest and try to figure out what we were doing. I was surprised my mother didn't ask us why we took so long. My wood was all around our big tree and it looked beautiful. I was so proud to see them everyday so we usually didn't cook with them until the season for planning. We began using the wood when we were really busy. My mom admired my beautiful work.

Sadly just two weeks after I finished collecting my wood for Winter to come, that is when we found out that our names came out in Kampala, and we were to leave our home for America. All of the work we did and my mom staying all day to make sure we had food was seemingly for nothing. We ended up giving it away, and we had a short time to say goodbye to friends and everybody we knew in the village. I did not even have enough time to say goodbye to everybody. On January 17th, we left the refugee camp that was our home for fifteen years. Then on January 20th, we said goodbye to Africa, and we arrived in Idaho on January 21st at 5 PM.

What went wrong

It was in 1987, in South Sudan, when the war became worse. The village was destroyed and people left their homes for safety in border countries, like Uganda, Kenya, Ethiopia, or the Democratic Republic of Congo (DRC). A lot of lives were lost and families weret separated. That was the second Sudanese civil war (1983-2005.) The Sudanese had their first war in (1955-1972) the year my mother was born, and it was a seventeen-year conflict between the Northern and Southern regions of Sudan.

The war began a year before Sudan declared independence from Great Britain. The main belligerents in the war were the central government of Sudan and the Southern Sudan Liberation Movement (SSLM). Great Britain, Egypt, and the Soviet Union supported the central government.

While Ethiopia, Uganda, and Israel were supporting Southern regions. During this war, an estimated 500,000 people died.

The roots of the conflict can be traced to 1953, when the United Kingdom and Egypt agreed in 1956 that Sudan would become an independent nation. The South called themselves Equatoria and my Acholi people were included. They were composed mostly of British colonial soldiers from Southern regions. They attempted to disperse a crowd of protesters in the Town of Torit, Sudan (now it is South Sudan). The Southern soldiers appeared to be sympathetic to the protesters, they were prompting the central government in Khartoum (the capital of Sudan) to place them with troops from the northern region. The soldiers of Southern mutinied, and there was an estimated killing of 336 northerners both soldiers and civilians. The soldiers of Southern mutiny spread across Sudan revolted.

Religion also influenced the conflict. In the Northern two thirds of Sudanese people were overwhelmingly Muslim, while Christianity or indigenous religions were most popular in the south. Northern Sudanese people culturally spoke Arabic, and identified with Saudi Arabia and North Africa. The south identified with Ethiopia and the newly independent country nearby. As the fighting progressed, the south was the first to insurgency, and to recruit child soldiers. South Sudan rebels divided into two factors as the fighting continued.

One group, the Anya Nya, was founded and led by Joseph Lagu. The group was composed mostly of the Madi group, and The Sudan African National Union (SANU) was formed and led by William Deng from the Dinka ethnic group. Since the north was the government at the time, the northern forces were unable to put down the rebellion, several coups brought about new governments. Ten years after the Civil war began, prime Minister Muhammad Ahmad Mahgoub offered the southern Sudanese rebels to lay down their arms. The south rejected the offer and the fight continued.

In 1969, General Geaafar Nimeri took control of the Sudanese government. In 1972, the people who left Sudan were to return to their country. Some decided to stay in Uganda, but my family went back. Again, in 1983, the war between the government and the Rebel's began again. It remained until it reached our village and the people had to leave Sudan again. That fight continued until the year 2005. Sudan signed apeace agreement in Kenya on January 9, 2005, after twenty-two (22) years of conflict between the Central government in Khartoum and the people's Liberation Army (SPLA). About two million people died in the conflict, but the war led South Sudan becoming an independent nation in 2011.

The Spirit of Warriors: Never stop telling stories about your people to your children.

CHAPTER FIVE

Going Back Home

My first time going to South Sudan was in 2021, because I was born in Uganda. I decided to go through Uganda, Entebbe Airport, because of COVID, and it took me four days. I was on the way from Iowa to Chicago; from Chicago to Washington; from Washington to Brussels; from Brussels Belgium to Kigali Burundi; and from Kigali to Entebbe Uganda. It has been fifteen years since I came to the United States. I was exhausted, and my whole body hurt, but I was so excited! Finally, I was home.

There is something about going back to Africa, it doesn't matter how many times you go back. When back at home, you feel free, you feel welcome, you see your own people working at the airport, you speak the same language, you feel love, and nobody calls you black, or brown. It's funny, they call me American. American? I am African. The western world treated us differently. I don't like it, and it makes me sick to my stomach. I just want to be me, a beautiful, strong, African. My passport shouldn't define who I am in my own country, but it is what it is.

When I decided to become an American citizen, I swore to be American, but the feeling I get when I see my own people is incredible and lovely. We arrived at Entebbe at midnight, and we checked in at immigration for a visa. Everything took an hour. One of the family members were waiting for me. God bless his heart. We went from Entebbe straight to Bweyale, a city close to Gulu in Northern Uganda. I grew up in Bweyale, it is a peaceful place and dear to my heart.

We arrived in Bweyale at 6 AM

My auntie and I had a beautiful moment that morning. I was expecting to be with my sister Sabina, from Canada, but she couldn't make it because of COVID. We did everything together; we said we would live or die together, and we planned to go on this trip, my first trip back to Africa together. Sabina has always been there for me, and I love her dearly. She is not my real sister, but she's closer to me than any of my blood sisters.

We grew up together, and she is a tough young woman. I guess that's why I like her so much. She is also wise and we reason together a lot. It was a blessing for me to see her mother first thing in the morning. We talked, we cooked, we ate and laughed a lot. It was the kind of laughter that makes your stomach hurt and you can't stop, because you feel so good. That same day, I saw James. he came from South Sudan to meet me in Uganda, after having not seen me for over fifteen years. We have been in communication and we planned to go to South Sudan together. He was living in Juba, the Capital of South Sudan. It was a moment I will never forget. Sixteen years after we said goodbye to one another, there we were talking. We talked on the phone for ten years, then face to face, once again. God is good.

The Spirit of Warriors: You never give up on what God put in your heart.

GOING TO KITGUM

Kitgum is a City in Northern Uganda. We left Kitgum when I was a baby. I didn't remember anything about Northern Uganda while I was growing up. I heard that the rebels were in Northern Uganda. All of the horrible things that we heard that the rebels were doing, could keep you awake all night. Now, there I was going through the Acholi land.

Northern Uganda and South Sudan didn't have much peace yet. I was going through this place, and it was breathtaking for me, looking at the beautiful place God created. God's chosen people, a tear fell down my eyes.

We spent about two hours there because the car broke down and the driver was fixing the car. I am not sure if he knew what he was doing, but for me it was divine synchronicity. We arrived in Kitgum at 8:30 PM. Good thing the driver knew my sister and took us all the way home. Kitgum is a beautiful place. I would say the hills are like California, if Uganda continues to develop, Kitgum could be one of the best cities in Uganda. I am not saying this because I was born there. It's because I feel connected with the place in all kinds of ways. Kitgum is my comfort place in this world.

The Spirit of Warriors is always connected to itself.

MEETING MY DAD

So many children in this world have a strange relationship with their fathers. I am one of them. My mom and dad had an ugly divorce and they didn't speak to each other or co-parent my siblings and me. The last time I talked to my father, I believe I was five years old. I don't remember calling him dad nor do I recall calling anyone dad in my whole life. My step-father was a wonderful man, but I never had the desire to call him father. He taught me what a good man should be like. After 28 years, I finally got to meet my father and talk to him face to face.

I was excited and nervous at the same time. My sister was doing all of the shopping. I wish I knew something about my dad and could have bought him clothes from America. When my sister and I got to my dad, he made note of the clothes she got him from Kitgum right away. That was when

I learned my dad doesn't like cheap things. He asked, "Where are the clothes you brought me from America?"

He said, "Who is going to wear these cheap clothes from Kitgum?" I was surprised, because he said he was blind now. He couldn't see, but he knew everything. He even told me that when I was a baby he lost hope because I was sick all of the time. He asked how I became the tallest and most beautiful among my sisters. I was laughing and confused a little. I thought my father couldn't see. We spent all night talking and laughing, my father was a comedian. I hated to see what alcohol did to him, but for sure, he was a happy man.

The Spirit of Warriors: Be happy with yourself.

MY MOTHERLAND

Have you heard of the song Mama Land by Yvonne Chaka Chaka? There are three lines I got from the song, "Please stop fighting, please stop killings and we better unite for mama land." My journey from Kampala going through East North of Uganda from all those small cities and villages, makes me see the beauty of our land.

When we were leaving my dads, we were going to a place called Pajok in South Sudan, where my mother was born. It was my first time stepping foot on South Sudan land. The road was so bad that the car could not go through. We had to take a motorcycle. It was supposed to be a three hour journey, but we spent all day on the road. As soon as we got on the border, and I stepped foot in the land of South Sudan, all of the clouds became so dark. It was one of those rains that you could see from the hills and hear coming towards you.

It was stunningly beautiful, and everyone was going for shelter. I wanted the rain to touch me. I wanted the rain to welcome me. For me, rain is a promise from God. Rain, for me, is God saying, "I am keeping my promise for you and your people, It is like God is choosing to bring peace in South Sudan. I have had this connection to South Sudan since I was young. Every time I hear bad news about Sudan, my heart deeply troubles me. In those moments, I imagine that I am this chosen leader to bring peace to South Sudan, and when I say something, people will listen.

I was lost in my thoughts, when my sister grabbed my hand to escort me to a small hut. The wall wasn't finished all the way, so half of it stood strong and welcomed us and while we are sitting inside, we can see everything outside. While everyone was talking and laughing, I grabbed my sister's hand and held it tight. I asked God one question, "What do you want me to do in South Sudan before my time ends in this world?" I heard the answer: Peace.

The spirit of a warrior is to be willing to die for the cause - Nelson Mandela

A Journey to my mother village.

We sat at the border for hours. After the rain, we had to continue with the journey. I asked the Lord to have mercy on us, because the roads were so muddy. The motorcycle couldn't go anywhere, and we had to walk. My sister went ahead of us, and my best friend James was behind us. I was in the middle. This was my first time walking alone on a long road in South Sudan. I was afraid to sit on the motorcycle because the driver kept falling. The road was so slippery.

The motorcycle went ahead of me. Oh this is great, I will just follow the motorcycle trail and hope to make it home. Soon, I found my sister waiting for us at the South Sudan immigration office. It was about four or six small huts in the middle of nowhere. They must stamp our papers for us to enter South Sudan. I was so tired, I just wanted to have a warm shower and a good bed. This is something we take for granted in America.

I asked my sister how much more time do we have left, and she said not a lot, about two to three hours before we should be home. She just said it like that was nothing. They walk all the time, but for me, I was dead already. I had no choice but to continue walking again. Believe me, I don't care how much exercise I do in America. When you go to Africa, you will lose weight without dieting. By the time we got home, I was about ten pounds lighter.

My auntie Rose wanted me to step into an egg before entering the home. Seriously, I can't even lift my leg, but it's a tradition, so I must. I can't describe the feeling I get when I see my family. We were soaking wet and muddy, but no one cared! I was home at last. I was home in Pajok. I finally crossed the Atepi river.

The Spirit of Warriors: If it doesn't kill you, do it.

MY JOURNEY TO JUBA

We spent three days in Pajok and with my relatives, cooking, eating, and going to collect water from Atepi river. I went around the place, I visited a school and a hospital. People were coming back home after the tribal fight in 2018, and this is a problem we have in South Sudan. Everything will start to go well and people will be focusing on building their homes when suddenly a war will begin for a stupid reason. People lost their homes and family members. They find themselves in Uganda again, starting all over repeatedly since 1872. It is old, and people are tired of the stupid life cycle in South Sudan. It has happened to my mom's generation, my generation, and now in my kid's generation. The people of South Sudan have had enough of this, and our time is now, to step up, and say no more.

The scripture 1 Peter 3:12 says: For the eyes of the Lord are on the righteous, and his ears are open to their prayer. But the face of the Lord is against those who do evil. This verse is speaking directly to the people of South Sudan. There are those who are crying for peace and there are those who are doing evil, but think they have the right to do so. Their eyes are blind. This is why I said the people of South Sudan may become independent again from the North, but they will not be free from their minds. Everything in South Sudan is "I" and "my."

As we left my mom's village going through Obbo, Magwi and Panyikwara, I saw the need in our community. There was no good hospital, no good school no good church, and the people looked worn out with life. There were so many young girls at the age of fourteen with babies, and they can't take care of themselves. I saw people coming from their gardens, carrying their hoe with such exhausting movement. I feel for them, and I wished I could do something.

There was so much needed in South Sudan, and when I entered the capital of South Sudan, right away, I didn't like it. "How can people live in this place?" I asked James. It is congested with so many cars and people, it's like, everybody from South Sudan is in Juba. It's hot, from the bridge to Gudele, it should take twenty to thirty minutes to drive, but it took us two to three hours. I tell myself, I love South Sudan, but I will never live in Juba. I lived there for four days, and my skin was dry. I felt horrible. I wish the government could move the capital of South Sudan elsewhere besides Juba.

I believe we have started the movement, but it will take generations for the work to be completed. It is just like the children of Israel. God made them spend forty years in the desert, until all the generations from Egypt passed away because of their minds.

Joshua 5:6 says that the Israelites traveled in the wilderness for forty years and remained until the death of the men who were of military age when they left Egypt. This happened because they had not obeyed the LORD. For the LORD had sworn to them that they would not see the land he had solemnly promised their ancestors. To give them a land flowing with milk and honey. I am not a prophet and God did not speak to me directly, but history repeats itself. I believe this is what is going to happen in South Sudan.

The Spirit of Warriors does not quit until they see the promise come to pass.

CHAPTER SIX

Living As A Refugee

What is one word that comes to your mind when you hear the word *refugee*? Pain, suffering, hardship, poverty, disadvantage, insufficient? I was watching a documentary by Reggie Yates. He went to Iraq to spend six days with the refugees from Syria, and he asked the question, "Do you just help each other here for free?" The man answered and said, "We are all in the same situation here, and all we have here is what we got." I can surely relate to him. As humans, we are animals that can think and do. No matter how bad the situation is, we either get used to it, find a way out of it, or find joy and love in it.

When people ask me how my life was in a refugee camp, and ask me to describe the feeling, I think, "Yes, yes, I can. I felt joy and love, peace and care." I was born in a refugee camp, and lived there for fifteen years before coming to America. That is the only life I know. Dr. Myles Munroe said: a man doesn't know he is poor until he meets a rich man. I believe it is the same thing with every single human being on earth. I didn't know my life was bad until I came to America. There, I started to hear the word refugee. When I was living in that camp, I was used to it. We didn't know, we were refugees, and that speaks to the power of the mind.

Human beings can train their mind to believe anything they want it to believe. Our refugee camp called Kiryandongo was one of the best camps in Uganda. They decided to give a plot to every family, and we had clean water, schools, a hospital, churches, a market, and a community. Human's basic needs are food, water, clothing, sleep, and shelter. We got all those and more. Life was easy at the beginning. When people start working in their gardens and growing their own food, life becomes much easier.

I remember my mom and others would form groups to work together in their garden. About thirty people would come together, and write numbers on small pieces of paper. They crumbled the paper into small pieces and everyone picked a piece. Whatever number you got would determine when it would be your turn for people to come to your garden. You'd have to provide food, water, and homemade alcohol. They worked hard, and they didn't forget to have fun after the hard labor all day in the garden. If the food or alcohol didn't taste that great, you'd be fined and would have to give valuable items or money to the group.

Men had their group, and women had their group. The youth had their own groups as well, and everyone was dedicated to doing their very best. This always made me so happy to think about it. There we were living in the camp, and no one had formal education. Yet, people learned the power of collaboration and union. They learned to support each other and left no one behind. Unless you were lazy. We have one of those in every community or country. I am so glad I learned these lessons my mother's generation passed on to us.

A refugee is defined as a person who has been forced to leave their country to escape war, persecution, or natural disasters. To the refugees, I say, think of that definition the next time someone asks you, or makes you feel like less because you lived in a refugee camp before going to America. Do not be ashamed of it. It's going to the school of life, studying hardship and how to overcome it. I know you learned the same. If you can leave your country, go through all the trauma and still remain standing, why not stand higher, and let the world see your light?

The enemy will not mess with you, unless he knows you've got something special. So, before you start thinking negatively about a refugee, consider your life. Your version of being a refugee could be the loss of family members, loss of positive thinking, because you married the wrong person, or lack of self-confidence. All of these experiences can cause you to end up in a bad environment.

The Spirit of Warriors: Think first about your life before judging others.

CHAPTER SEVEN

Coming To America

Imagination Similar: The ability of the mind to be creative or resourceful. Can you manifest your imagination into your reality and live it?

It was 2001, when we were about to start our process of coming to America. My sister Layet went to America in 1999, and she said she wanted us to come so we could get an education and a "good life." I remember talking to her on the phone. She said, "Are you ready to come to America?" "America?" "Yes, America." She replied, and continued, "You will be going to school on the bus, we have juice in the house, and there is food everywhere. You don't have to wait for mango season to come, you can eat mongo whenever you feel like it. You will never have to get up in the morning and go collect water, or wood for cooking."

I really liked the sound of that. I was quiet, and just said okay. My imagination was far gone. I thought about walking on gold roads, cutting bananas from our backyard, and putting a glass at the bottom of the fruits for passion fruit or any fruit juice to fill my glass. I thought about walking along the road where there was no dust, everyone is so happy, there's no more pain and suffering, free at last. I heard my mom call me to finish cooking, and after cooking, I had to go collect water for showers. I snapped out of my imagination, but everything seemed to be so real.

Before my sister went to America, when I was nine years old, I was home alone. All of the adults were at work in the garden, all of the children were at school, and my youngest sister was at my older sister's house. I couldn't go to school, because my mother could not pay for us all. Also, I was always sick, so I had to stay home. I couldn't walk the long mile to school.

Since I was always home, I helped take care of our family's livestock. We had goats, pigs and chickens. They became my friends. I was small and skinny, and some of our goats were big, when I untie them, I couldn't control them. I figured out how to get them to listen to me. I'd talk to them. I said to the big male one, "If you want to eat, don't drag me around if I untie you. Otherwise, I can't take you out to eat."

I looked him straight in the eye. He got the message and all of the animals became so humble towards me. When I took them out one day, I was sitting under a big tree. I believe the temperature was about 80 degrees. I remember it was a beautiful day. While I was sitting there, I saw a plane way up in the sky. I imagined myself being on that plane going somewhere beautiful. I hadn't seen the world yet and my imagination was going.

After I talked with my sister and she told me all of the beauty of America, it opened up my imagination and made me want to explore the world. I was feeling so good. A week after talking with my sister, we had to go to Kampala for an interview.

It was my first time leaving camp. We all packed up and two of my older sisters came with us. My mom didn't want to come to America. She said it would be great if my older sister, her firstborn, could replace her, that would be great. To get to America, we had to go through an interviewing process that could take up to a year. My older sister tried to remember all of the questions, but she couldn't so mom had to do it. My mom didn't go to school, but she is smart.

When we arrived in Kampala, there was no place prepared for us. We didn't get into the city until 7 PM. My family arranged to sleep at my aunty's house, then find us a place in the morning. There were nine of us going to my aunty's house. My uncle was renting it for her. The house was ten feet twenty, very small, and only her twin bed fit in there. As soon as we entered the gate, the woman who owned the place followed us.

She wanted to know who we were and where we were going to stay. My mom pleaded to let us spend the night inside her gate and said we would leave early in the morning. We just came from the village and have nowhere to go this late. She agreed, but she wanted us out of there by 10 AM. Mom said thank you, and then we had to find what we would sleep on that night.

I can tell my aunty was not so happy with us all being there. I don't remember eating anything that day, or aunty giving us something to eat. On the other hand, we were only there an hour and my brother was already in this man's house watching TV with them. I remember sitting by the door. The man was very kind, but my brother did not want me to go in there.

I sat by the door and watched for about two minutes, then I got a knock on my head to leave the place. For two minutes, I didn't understand what they were saying, but there was a woman in a long dress doing something important. The children were clapping their hands for her. It was so beautiful, it left me deep in thought.

We spent the night sleeping outside. Early in the morning as promised, my sister's brother-in-law came to get us. We went to his mom's place, and he and my mom went to look for places to stay. By 1 PM, they found a place for us. It was a house with two rooms, and it was enough room for everyone to sleep inside the house.

The man we rented from had two older daughters. They were so beautiful. They could not continue with their education because he couldn't afford it. So they turned to the streets to make a living, selling their bodies. One got pregnant, and the baby passed away after she was a month or so old.

They had to bury her in the junk place at night, because they couldn't afford to buy the cemetery spot. It was very sickening for me. City life looked so strange to me. At least they had an avocado tree. We'd look forward to hearing it fall at night. Whoever heard it could go get it. That was a lot of fun for us kids.

We stayed in Kampala for a week, and we went to the interview on Tuesday. Mom did a great job! She passed the interview, and they didn't ask us kids. We just stayed in the waiting room for mom. As we waited, we sat by the door so we could see outside. We were there all day. At around 4 PM, kids began coming from school. They'd pass by with other people, and look at us like what are they doing?

When we got home, mom asked if we heard what those kids were saying. I said no, because I did not speak their language. My mom grew up in Uganda. Her family ran to Uganda when she was a little girl. She can speak Swahili, and a little bit of Buganda and Arabic. My mom said one of the boys asked his friend, "What are those people doing in this office?" One of them answered and said, those are the people that are bought by America, and they are going to clean horse's teeth.

We laughed about it, but mother wasn't laughing. I knew she really didn't want to come to America, but she sacrificed herself, her husband, and her family for us. After a week, we had to go back to camp, because we couldn't afford to live in the city. This went on for about a year. Until one day, our name came on the board. We were so happy, we were leaving Uganda on September 25th, 2001. We were to be in Kampala on September 18th, but we got a call on September 12th, telling us not to go to Kampala.

All of the flights were canceled. America was attacked, and everything was canceled until further notice. Okay, now what? We had to go back to school and start life all over again. In 2003 we went back and forth to Kampala, and in 2004, we gave up.

We went back to our normal lives. We weren't thinking about America. After a hot day in January of 2005, Mom was in the garden, and me and my little sister were home. We saw Oriya on a bicycle coming toward our home. He was my brother's friend. We did an interview together, but they didn't pass their interview. He asked where mom was, and I told him that she was in the garden. He told me that when mom gets home, I should tell her our family name was on the board in Kampala. Our family was to leave the following week.

We began jumping with excitement and joy. I couldn't believe it. After five years, we were finally going to America. We did not have time to say goodbye to all of our relatives, but I remember going as fast as I could to James' friend's house. I went to let him know we were leaving in four days. I wanted to tell James to come on Saturday. That was the day we were having a party to say goodbye to all of our family and friends.

James, was a boy I really liked. We started talking, but it wasn't serious. We were young and if my mom found out I was talking to a boy at 14 years old, I would've been dead. She would not kill me, but she would beat me and a long lesson would have taken place.

On the day of the celebration, we were free to do whatever. The same day, there was a dance at the local market. They set these things up in the community so young adults could have fun. It was like a club, but people danced out when their parents allowed it. I wasn't allowed to go yet, because my mom thought I was still too young. However, that night, she allowed me.

I was so happy, but I knew I wasn't going to dance. I wanted to talk to James. His friend arranged everything for us. I thought that was a bit too much, because in my mind, I just wanted to talk to him, and say goodbye. I guess he had a different plan. His friend gave him a hut for us to hang out in. In our place, when a boy turns sixteen, they could build their own hut to sleep in, so they won't have to share space with their siblings.

After I found out what James was thinking, I lied to him. I told him I was not ready, but that I would be the next day. He agreed, but that was the last time he would say goodbye to me. I lied because in my mind, I didn't want to have sex with a boy until we got married. I wanted to be married on a higher level, and be taken to my husband's house with pride.

NEW YORK

That Sunday morning, we left the refugee camp. We spent two days in Kampala, and on a Tuesday night, we left Uganda. When we got on the plane, there were four hundred passengers and most of them were white people. I was confused, I had never seen that many white people in Uganda. Where did they come from? I was curious. We had a Case Worker from Uganda to Europe. To the Netherlands Amsterdam Airport, from Amsterdam, he helped us to our next flight to New York.

He said goodbye and another Case Worker was waiting for us in New York. I noticed the food was different from the Netherlands to New York. The soda tasted different, and we didn't understand the name of the food. I remember getting fried chicken, salad, and Pepsi. I recall the blue can. I tasted the chicken, and I didn't like it. I tried the salad, and I didn't like it. I tried the soda, but it didn't taste like African soda.

My brother was sitting next to me, and he ate his food and all of my food! I looked at him like, how do you like this food? We arrived at John F. Kennedy International Airport at night. I was wearing a short skirt that stopped at my knee, a t-shirt, and slippers. Imagine this poor mother with six children in New York City in January, in summer clothes. Everyone looked at us like they wondered where we came from. Not from America, I can tell you that.

Our Caseworker, a beautiful African-American woman, wore long brown and black pants and boots. She was thick, medium-sized, with long black hair. She began with my brother and shook our hands with a warm smile. When she got to me, I was stunned. Looking at her, I thought, wow, can a woman do this? I was amazed looking around the airport, I saw women of every color, shape, and profession. They all seem to be so busy going up and down. I wanted to be like them, they looked so free.

In my heart, I thought to myself, I want to be like those women when I grow up. Our Caseworker, whose name I don't remember, was so kind. She asked my mom if she could adopt one of us. She looked like she was in her forties and said she didn't have kids. I kept looking at her, and she walked with such confidence. I loved her and I wanted to be like her. She was so helpful, she took us to our hotel rooms. After we settled in our rooms, thirty minutes later the hostel worker brought us fried chicken and soda. I personally thought it was a turkey leg because the leg was giant, and those did not look like chicken legs. Whatever it was, was not a normal size.

We traveled with an elderly woman, and because of her age and out of respect, we called her grandma. She also had an assigned case worker. Her case worker traveled with her from Uganda because she doesn't write or speak English. Because her caseworker was a male, my brother shared a room with him. The grandma was lonely and started crying, so my mom made sure my sister Roselyn and I stayed with her. We slept in the same room on two beds, and grandma felt better. Poor grandma was just looking at the chicken. I don't remember seeing her eat. Grandma was so miserable.

After eating, Roselyn and I were looking through the window. New Years had passed twenty days prior, and they hadn't taken down all of the Christmas lights from the tree.

It looked so beautiful, and was a white and blue color around the hotel. Everything looked so different and unique to us. Early in the morning, the Caseworker showed up. I don't remember which state grama was going to, but for us, our Case Worker took us on a plane to Denver, Colorado.

We said goodbye to her, and when we arrived in Denver, someone was there to connect us to Boise, Idaho, where my sister and her family were.

We arrived at Boise Airport at 5 PM. My sister, was there with her friend and some of our relatives to welcome us to the U.S. It was a beautiful feeling, they took us to our new home. My sister and her friend cooked a lot of food to welcome us. We didn't have many problems, because we had a family to help us. We also had the Caseworker for medical appointments and within one month we started school. My sister Roselyn and I started school at Riverside Elementary for about three months, then we went for summer break, and stayed at home for three months.

After the summer, I started high school at Centennial High school on the West side of Boise. My sister and her husband bought a new home on the west side, and my sister Stella and I were leaving with my sister to help her with the babysitting. She had one son and one was on the way.

My sister Layet and her husband Kennedy were both going to school and working. Us coming to the U.S helped them a lot. The idea was for my mom to help them babysit their kids while they went to school, but mom said no. She said she didn't come to America to sit home and do nothing, she wanted to work, or they must take her back home. My mom is a no-joke woman.

The Spirit of Warriors: Be curious about everywhere you go. Remember your journey and take notes.

CHAPTER EIGHT

Starting High School

I began high school and did not speak English at the time. High school was fun but not speaking English made it difficult. I started learning my ABCs in ninth grade. We had our English as a Second Language (ESL) classroom outside of a big building. They built a mobile home by the school compound and every kid from a different country had to go there. We had students from Mexico, Russia, Ukraine, Japan, Somalia, China, and South Sudan. We all came from different parts of the world, but we all had one mission to have a better life.

We were all at different levels of education as well. Some had been in America for two years, some had been for years, and others, like me, had been in America less than a year. We didn't speak good English, but we understood each other. No one made fun of anyone or laughed at anyone if they made a mistake.

Our teacher was from Ukraine. Her name was Nina Sloan. She was about five foot two, had beautiful long dark brown hair, and had the most beautiful soul. She cared so deeply about every single one of us. She took her job seriously, and she was more than a teacher to us. She was the mother of every child would have liked to have.

I remember some of the boys were not nice to her and they made her cry. I was heartbroken, I didn't understand why they would do such a thing. She was devoted to helping us all succeed in life. I think the school was not ready to take all of us kids. She was one teacher with part-time help, and every student had different needs. She was not getting the help that she needed.

Just like in every part of America, people really didn't understand how to welcome refugees when they arrived. Every country is different, so that meant every student was different, and they all required special needs. One person in school couldn't handle it all. My heart goes out to every single ESL teacher worldwide.

My first classes for the semester were ESL, computer, and English reading. There were three students in the class, Jose from Mexico, he wanted to be a police officer, a girl from Russia, who wanted to be a teacher, and I was from Uganda, and wanted to be a doctor. I wanted to be a doctor, because I wanted to help people. I wanted to build a hospital in South Sudan. I knew what I wanted, but I needed to know how to get there. If teachers can take their little time and invest in the refugee children, you'd be amazed by what those children could do.

 It doesn't matter how big the dream is, if God puts it in their heart, encourage them, and go out of your way to connect them with the right people. I told my teacher about my dream, and she didn't kill it. Instead, she said being a doctor is not easy and that I should try something like a nurse. All I can say is she knew what she knew. When refugees come to the Western world, they are determined to do whatever it takes to better their life. Anything is possible for them. For me, I thought it was, and I lived by it every day. I might not be a doctor yet, but check on me ten years from now.

The world we lived in, we were all looking for peace and a good life. I believe if we all learned how to help each other in some way, we could create this beautiful world that we all want to live in. How can we do that? By giving those who are willing to put in the work the opportunity. If I become wealthy, the government and community will benefit from me, and I will have opportunities to share with others who are willing to do the work.

As I continued with my school after one year, I began to take more classes in a regular class, but I still needed a lot of help. Mrs. Sloan was overwhelmed with all the students asking for help and new students kept arriving. Some of us who were in the country for a year were being left behind.

My mom was stressed out as well, because after six months, all of the help was gone. She had to go to work and the money was not enough to support us. My brother couldn't continue with his education because he was past High school age and Boise did not have anything to support Him with his education in 2006. He was stressed out and began drinking alcohol more and more. He started getting into trouble with the law, and now all of this money was going to legal fees for a charge of Driving Under the Influence(DUI).

Mom wanted me to get a job and help her, because we started to get the bills for the immigration office. My family owed immigration eleven thousand dollars. Education became secondary to us. When I turned seventeen in America, my real age was fifteen. People had this idea that when you increase your age, you'd retire early to enjoy life. Age problems mess up a lot of people. We call it a Sudanese birthday. Everyone chose January first. None of us knew our real birthdays. America was kind and gave us all January first.

My first Job was at Walmart as a cashier. I woke up at 5:30 AM. I had to go get my mom, because she worked overnight at Walmart. I dropped her off at home, and got ready to go to school. I came from school at 3:30 PM, left my books at home, and got ready to go to work from 5 - 9 PM. Then I rushed home, picked my mom up, dropped her off at work, then came home, tried to do my homework, fell asleep, then got up and started it all over again. That became my life.

The pressure of life became too much. I really didn't want to get married. I wanted to continue with my education, but just like most of the women out there, I met a man, Joe. Talking to Joe gave me some comfort. I told him I didn't want to get married now. I told him I wanted to continue with my education. He said no problem, but told me that if I had his baby I could continue with my education. I knew that was a stupid idea. If I couldn't take care of myself, how could I care for a child? Nothing was making sense. In February of 2007, he came to see me. I lied to my mom, and told her we had a school trip. This was a moment that changed my life forever.

The Spirit of Warriors: It's ok to fail, but don't give up. You can live the American dream.

CHAPTER NINE

Pregnant At Sixteen

On February 13th 2007, Joe came from Utah to see me. He picked me up from school. At my American age, I was already eighteen years old. Everyone began treating me like an adult. I was really only sixteen. When we met up, we had sex. I was not sure whether there was love or not. I didn't know what intimate partner love was.

I was looking for comfort. I wanted someone to listen to me and help, but I did not want to be someone's wife. Joe was probably in his thirties in his real age, but twenty-six years old in American age. This was the fun thing about this American age, some people went over, and some went under. Nobody knew their real age or the year some people were born.

In his mind, Joe was ready to have a wife, and he knew our culture. When you get a girl pregnant, they have to go with you because the parents will kick the girl out. Whether you like it or not, women had no choice or voice. This is why he said, if I wanted to continue with my education, I should have his child. He wasn't ready to be a father, but because of community pressure, he wanted a wife.

This is one thing I don't like about my community. When you are over twenty years old, everyone expects you to get married. They don't understand the meaning of getting married. I would say 99% of my people get married either because of family problems, or the community telling them that they are getting too old. It's so sad for us who are in America. Things have changed since the days of my grandparents. Things have changed since the days of my Mom and Dad. In the earlier years, a woman and a man come together to have children and build a community. A woman's dream was to get a husband and have children. Now, a woman does not need a man to fulfill her dreams, and life is not all about getting married and having a baby.

My message for the youth is to make sure you're your own wife before you become someone's wife. I will explain more about this later. On March 6, 2007, my life turned upside down. Here is the thing with family, when a girl gets pregnant, they take it personally as though you've hurt them. What they don't understand is that you are hurting more than anyone else. A week passed and I wasn't feeling well. I decided to go to the doctor, and one hour later, the doctor came and said you are pregnant.

Everything went blank. I don't remember anything else that the doctor said. I went to my car, and I sat in the parking lot for three hours. I was trying to figure out what to do. Should I go home? No! Should I go to my sister's house? No! I saw my school from the parking lot, and thought, should I go to school and maybe talk with Mrs. Sloan? No! I sat and cried and cried.

Finally, I gained some confidence and went to my sister's house. She was home. She works at night, around 2 PM, and she just woke up. I went to her room and told her. One thing with my sister, I couldn't tell if she was mad. I don't remember if she said anything to me. I left her house and went home.

The drive from my sister's house to our home was about ten minutes, but I felt like it was an all-day drive. When I got home, mom was sleeping. I went straight to our room, me and my two sisters shared a room. I couldn't go to work or school. I laid on my bed all day and night. I started to have all kinds of negative thoughts. I spoke with Joe, but the communication was not the same anymore. I was so mad at him. I told him I wanted to use protection, and he said no, don't worry about it. He told me I was still young and would not get pregnant, and I believed him.

Knowledge is key to life. If you don't have knowledge, people will play with your life, like a ball. The scripture, 1 Corinthians 8: 11, says and so by your knowledge this person is destroyed, the brother for whom Christ died. Joe thought he had knowledge to use against my will. Tricking someone young to fulfill your needs is an evil thing to do to young souls, because not everyone is strong enough to get out of the situation.

The Spirit of Warriors: Play fair with people, because your actions might destroy someone's future.

CHAPTER TEN

Kicked Out of the House

I was lying down in my room two days after I talked to my sister, when I heard the doorbell ring. It was my sister. She and my mom were sitting in the living room, and they started talking. I heard her ask mom, "Do you know why your daughter is sick?" My mom said, "No." I've been sick a lot over the years because since I started my period, every time I'm having my period each month, I'd get really bad pain.

I stayed home from school. I stayed home from school every month for two days or so. My mom already got used to me staying home when I'd get my period. My sister said, "Well, did she tell you she's pregnant?" Everything went quiet and my mind completely went blank. I did not hear everything that they said. The last thing I saw was my mom standing by the door. She did not say anything, but she just gave me a look.

If you know African mothers, you know that when they give you a look, their looks could kill you. Without a word, my mom gave me that look, that entire night. The next day she told my brother what happened, and my brother called me downstairs from my room. He did not say anything or ask me how I was doing. Nothing! He gave me 24 hours to get out of the house or I would see what would happen to me. I wasn't sure what he was going to do, because we were in America, but if this was in Africa, I could have been beaten.

The girls would be beaten so badly when they got pregnant back in Africa. I knew that I had to get out of the house, but I didn't know how and I didn't know when. I started thinking about it. I thought about getting out of the house, into my car, driving on the highway, and driving off of the highway to kill myself. I thought I should just take drugs and commit suicide. That is what was going on in my mind because at that point, I really felt like my life was over.

I was done. I didn't even want to think about anything anymore. My mom and family had this idea that they could just kick me out of the house, or Joe and his family would have to come and sit down to talk to my family. Joe will have to pay some dowry for what he has done, and usually, that's what they do.

Within a month, Joe came with his family. They sat down, they talked, and I guess it solved everything. They gave me a week to get out of the house to go to Joe's house. I guess they finished whatever they were talking about. Young women don't have a voice when they get pregnant. They don't ask you if you love the man or if you want to be with him. All of the decisions were made by parents on behalf of your life.

They acted like you didn't need to know. You don't even know how much the man paid for your dowry either. As a young girl, my only voice was to say yes and go. All they needed was money from him. Nobody was there to ask me anything, or ask if I loved him. I felt so alone, it was like I committed a crime.

My brother didn't talk to me for two years. All he worried about was that I would bring shame to the family. I was sixteen-years-old, I didn't know any better. In fact, nobody talked to me about sex. Children can just grow up and know nothing. The Bible said: Train up a child in the way he should go, and when he is old, he will not depart from it.

The Spirit of Warriors: Take ownership of your children until they are independent. As parents, you will have freedom when they are gone.

CHAPTER ELEVEN

Forced Into Marriage

The headline read: BBC A new UNICEF report released on Monday, March 8, 2021; suggests millions more underage girls are at risk of being forced into marriage around the world due to the coronavirus pandemic. It continues; According to UNICEF estimates, even before the pandemic struck, it was predicted that 100 million children would have been forced into marriage in the next ten years. Now that figure is even higher, with a projected ten percent (10%) increase.

This issue, when you read about it in the news, looks like something far away from you. When you are in the U. S., you think that way, but when you are in a country like South Sudan, it becomes normal to you. Everywhere you look, there are young girls with babies. When I went to Africa, my own niece, who was fourteen years old, had a one-year-old baby. My uncle's daughter was fifteen-years-old with a two-month-old baby. I was sixteen-years-old in America with the baby, and my mom was fifteen-years-old, when she had my older sister in 1970.

If my mom talked to me, I would say that was in the 70s, but now we are talking about child brides increasing in the next ten years. This is an issue that we can't ignore anymore. There's a saying that says it takes a village to raise a child. We have forgotten about that village. Teachers in the classroom are overwhelmed, single mothers are overwhelmed, single fathers are overwhelmed. The community is overwhelmed, and the country is overwhelmed by children's issues.

I went to a conference back in March about the workforce. The man that was talking said, "Straight forward in the next ten years after the baby boomers are all f*** up!" I thought there had to be a solution somehow. The next speaker was Steve Bench. His topic was "Attracting Tomorrow's Talent with Today's Leaders." Thank you, Steve!

I am a strong believer that the world belongs to us. Whatever we do today will affect our future for tomorrow. We as parents are too busy chasing money, while the enemy is busy catching our children. I am guilty of not having enough time with my children. Therefore, I tell you, do not worry about your life, what you will eat or drink; or about your body, what you will wear. Is not life more than food, and the body more than clothes? Look at the birds of the air; they do not sow or reap or store away in barns, and yet your heavenly Father feeds them. Are you not much more valuable than they? Matthew 6: 25-26 (NIV).

I always wondered what went wrong after all these wonderful things our Father promised us. If we can take the name religion out of the bible, I think we can be more open to learning from it, and really live the life that was chosen for us. God is not a Father of religion, He is King of this Kingdom and we are chosen to be His children to treat every human being with dignity and equal rights for all humankind. Those girls have more talent and the ability to make the world a better place. Forcing young girls to marry is like putting a person in Prison for crimes they did not do.

I knew I didn't commit a crime, but kicking me out of the house, without even taking the time to ask what happened took my self-esteem out of me. My confidence was gone, and I felt lost and confused. There is one thing that saved me, my ESL teacher. I went to say goodbye to Mrs. Sloan, because she was like a mother to me, she introduced me to love and care, and she was the first person to give me a hug.

When a girl named Brenda called me a Monkey in my Art class, I was crying and hurt. Mrs. Sloan made me feel better at the moment. I needed it. When I went to say goodbye, she took me outside by the baseball field, we sat on the bench, and we talked for about two hours. She offered me the chance to stay in her house so I can finish High School. I was afraid, so I didn't take the offer.

Even though I didn't, she still loved me. She looked me straight into my eyes and said, "You have to remember what I am going to tell you. You are going to be a mother without an education, people will look down on you because you don't have an education. People will look down on you because you're a woman. People will look down on you because you are black, but don't ever let anyone look down on you, because you have no education, because you're a woman and because you are black. You can go back to school after the baby, you're a smart woman, and I believe you will do something great in this world."

I take that advice everywhere I've gone, no matter how bad life gets. I remember Mrs. Sloan's words. She didn't know me that deeply, but she took her time to let me know I mattered. We need more adults like Mrs. Sloan. If we want to reduce the increased number of girls being forced into marriage. One organization can't do it all. We all must stand up for our children. I am glad someone from Ukraine stood up for me. That's why you are reading my story. Will someone write your name in their book? Or appropriate your name on their achievements in life?

The Spirit of Warriors: It only takes one word to change someone's life.

CHAPTER TWELVE

My First Child

There are two mothers in the Bible, Elizabeth, the mother of John the Baptist, and Mary, the mother of Jesus. Elizabeth asked God for a baby, and Mary was chosen to be the Mother of Jesus. I found myself to be like Mary. I didn't choose to be a mother. I believe it was time for those boys to come into the world, and God chose me to bring them into this world. This is the principle I live by. Otherwise, I would have lost my mind believing someone took advantage of me when I was young.

I was done with that, it will do you no good. I found myself stuck and not going anywhere. Until I started to realize, everything that happens to us, bad or good, is allowed by the creator. As he said in Jerimiah 1:5, He knew us before we were in our mother's womb. That means, you can really change what hits you by surprise. Don't get me wrong, the man did take advantage of me. I was young and did not know any better, but why keep dwelling on the negative? Choose happiness and joy while you are still young.

When you are young, having a baby is not that difficult. I didn't put too much thinking into it, because I really didn't know what was going on with my body, or what to do. When the baby came, I wasn't worried about the baby swerving around, or the baby's future, I didn't even start to think about the future. I went to work, came home, cooked, and watched T.V. Slept, and started all over again the next day. We lived in a two-bedroom apartment with two of Joe's cousins. We had one room, no room for the baby.

It occurred to me that I was working, but we had no money to buy a baby crib. I have to borrow money from my mom to buy a crib and some clothes for our baby. I had no knowledge of life. I was this little girl, who was carrying a baby, and soon, the baby would come into this world with no good foundation.

On November 19th at around 11 PM. I started to get pain in my back. I told Joe I was having this pain, but it kept going away and coming back. He said not to worry about it, because the doctor said I was going to have the baby on December 5th. I didn't know. I got myself into bed, around 2 AM, but I could not sleep. The pain kept coming every ten minutes.

I called my sister, and she asked me how often the pain came. I said every ten minutes. She said if the pain started to come every five minutes, I should go to the hospital. Around 7 AM, I couldn't wait anymore. The hospital was about ten minutes from our home, but it felt like we were on the road for ten hours. We arrived in the Emergency Room and they took me to my room and called my doctor.

He came from his office across the street right away. I had to take all of my clothes off, and they asked me to lay on the bed. He put all of his hand into my private part, and when he took it out, he said, "Yah, you are having a baby today. You are eight centimeters." That was a painful moment. Why didn't I get all of this information before it was time to have the baby?

Someone could have said, oh by the way, since you are already pregnant, just know, when the pain starts, your water might break from home. By the way, a lot of liquid will come out of your private part. If not that, some women's pain starts with blood, the blood might start coming out from their private parts. You should not panic, but make sure to get to the hospital right away or call 911. If this happens, they start to lose blood very fast and they might need a blood transfusion.

Some women's pain starts every two hours or so, and keeps increasing with time. When you get to every ten minutes, make your way to a hospital, because that means you're about to have a baby! It would have been so helpful to me, if I knew this information. Well, nowadays, everything is on the internet and everyone has a smartphone. Please Google things and get all of the knowledge you can get. Ask questions too!

Our first son arrived on November 20th by 11:35. He was so beautiful and he looked just like me. Everybody in the hospital tried to help me. The nutritionist came in and they talked to me about breastfeeding and taking care of the baby. They told me what to expect when I got home, and what would happen when the baby cried. We talked about what I could do when the baby was not doing well and other things like this.

I just looked at them. I didn't remember every word they said, but I had knowledge from taking care of my sister, my nieces, and lots of babies when I was growing up. On Thanksgiving Day, we were discharged from the hospital. I didn't understand why the doctor or the nurse did not give me a painkiller or pain medication. They wrote a prescription, but when we got home, because of the Thanksgiving holiday, everything was closed.

We didn't even have pain medications at home. The pain that night was worse than the pain from having the baby. I was miserable and in so much pain. I was young and I did not know what to do. It didn't even occur to me to go to Walmart since they were open 24/7 and getting medicine from Walmart might lower my pain. I didn't think about any of that. Instead, I thought about getting the medication the next morning and I endured the pain until then. It was really painful.

Now, I really understand why the Bible says, my people perish because of lack of knowledge. It is not because of money or education, if you have the knowledge you think and give more consideration to things. I didn't have the knowledge or principles to be a mother, or knowledge to be a housewife. I didn't have any kind of knowledge to be that person that the man wanted me to be, because I was a baby. In his mind, he expected me to be this great mother who would really care for the baby well, keep up the house, and do everything.

I was sixteen. I couldn't even take care of myself and there I was with a baby. I didn't know what to do with this baby. I took care of my siblings in Africa, when you become a teenager, you take care of the house that helped you. I tell every single woman that if you are planning to be a mother, please take your time to read, and get the knowledge. Whether it's a planned pregnancy or not.

Children are a gift and it's a blessing. You can manifest in your child whatever you want them to be. I can really see the difference in each of my four boys. With my first born, I didn't have so much stress. I didn't think about life much, I just knew I was having a baby. My first born is a free thinker. His mind is completely different from my second child. I had to work hard to help my second and third children with their mindset. I was in a deep depression when I was pregnant with them. I almost lost my second child because of depression. I was in serious depression while in the relationship I was in, to the point where my whole body hurt. I was not in a position to be having a child whatsoever. That is how I lost my daughter.

How can you form a good life when you feel so lost? Once I had my fifth child, I gave up on the relationship. We were living together, but in different rooms. We went a year without meeting together. One night, I was on the phone with a male friend I grew up with. I love that boy. I began to have feelings for my friend on the phone. Since the man I loved was far away at the time, I turned to Joe. Just one night after a long time of not being with each other, I found myself pregnant.

This time I wasn't confused or anything. I knew I had to give the best life to this baby, a life the baby deserved. I went vegetarian. I practiced good thinking. I watched good things. I began listening to good preaching and motivational speaking. I was constantly putting something good in my brain. Now that he is born, he thinks differently. He believes differently. He is calm, he is loving and he likes hugging and affection.

The relationship I have with my first son is okay. I was there for him mentally and physically when he was in my womb, so we have a bond. It is a different kind of bond. My last one loves me freely, because I opened that door for him. My take on motherhood is that if you are planning to be a mother, take your time to study more about being the best mother you can be. Let us manifest what we want in them.

After they are born into this world and grow up, they are ready to face the world because of what you have done when they were in your womb. This is the love that all mothers should give their children. Our world can be a better place.

This is the Spirit of Warriors: Start developing your children when they're in your womb.

CHAPTER THIRTEEN

I Knew It Was
Not Going To Work

We arrived in Utah at around 6:00 PM and we went to Joe's uncle's house. We stayed there for about two hours, then we drove about twenty-five minutes to our apartment. I found Joe living with two of his cousins in a two-bedroom apartment. One bedroom was for him and I, and the other one for his cousins. Two grown men sharing a room. I was the only woman in the house. That night, I knew Joe and I would not be together, because even though I was laying in the bed with him, my mind, heart and soul was not there with him.

I didn't know what was happening. I really didn't want to be there. I did not want to be with this man, but because I was pregnant, I did not know how to leave. Just two weeks into the relationship, Joe slapped me. We were talking about getting up to pray so we could go to bed. I remember mentioning something about praying like a Muslim. I meant to say, he was bending down like a Muslim. Before I finished the sentence, I got repeatedly slapped in the face. That night, I slept on the floor and he didn't even have a heart to let me sleep in the bed because I was pregnant.

I wanted to get out, but where would I go? My brother didn't want me in our house and they kicked me out. I couldn't go back home. I felt stuck.

After a month or two, I got a job working in a store. I saved up some money, but the money was not enough for everything. When I met Joe and we started living together he was about $32,000 in debt. All of his money was going to pay off that debt.

He had a car loan and some other loans that he got. We were living paycheck to paycheck. We borrowed money for our rent and his bank account was in the negative. We had to pay a Payday loan fee, pay fees for the bank, and pay the rent. We were struggling. This man was in no position to get married or have a wife. Not to mention having a baby in this world.

When I started working, that helped a little bit. We still struggled with the money to buy food and money to support ourselves. We lived with roommates for a year, but our lease was up and everybody had to find their way. We found a one-bedroom apartment at the time. I went back to Idaho and Joe went to Africa, because his mother was sick.

His mother was sick for a long time. She was getting worse every day. He went to see her before she passed away. When he got back, I came back from Idaho. The struggle continued. We fought every day. Nothing made sense. We fought about everything.

One day we fought about my son having a fall. My son was a very active baby. He was learning how to walk so when he fell down, instead of me picking him up, I left him to help himself. Now Joe thought I shouldn't even let him fall. We had a big fight about our baby learning how to walk.

One day, Joe asked me to lay down. He got a belt and I thought it was a joke. I just started laughing. This is one of the dumbest things I have ever heard. Back in Africa, when a man asked a woman to lay down, they would beat their woman to death. I couldn't believe this man had a belt in his hand and asked me to lay down so that he could beat me. I was so confused. I did not know much, but that was something I could not do. I told him there is no way I would lay down. I told him if he tried to put his hands on me with that belt, we were going to fight.

That is what we did. We started fighting when he put his hands on me. Our life struggles continued. We moved into a two-bedroom apartment. After that, I got pregnant. I went back to high school, because I wanted to get my high school diploma and continue with my education. I attended Horizonte Institute and training center in Utah.

The struggle and the fighting continued. Doing my homework was a problem for Joe. When I found out I was pregnant with our second child, a girl, Joe was driving a taxi at the time. He spent most of his time in a parking lot. Joe thought that when he wasn't home, there was a man in his house, probably sleeping with me. I didn't understand Joe's brain, but that is what caused most of the problems in our home. He was so controlling and his self-doubt became my problem.

The Spirit of Warriors: Listen to your heart.

CHAPTER FOURTEEN

My Daughter

I was not really excited about being pregnant, but I was just living a life without purpose. I never really planned to have any of my children. I was eighteen and my focus was to go back to get my high school diploma so I could go to college. The school was filled with immigrants from every part of the world. It was a good opportunity to come to this country and start fresh.

I started going to the doctor and right away the doctor knew something was not right with the baby. He offered me two options. He said I could have an abortion or see a specialist at the University of Utah Hospital. When I got home, I told Joe and we both agreed that I would go to the University to see if there was anything they could do.

I spent all day in the hospital. I think I saw five to ten doctors that day. I had two different Magnetic Resonance Imaging (MRIs) done so they could see what was going on. They hadn't seen anything like it. My daughter had a heart defect. One in every four hundred thousand babies have it in the U.S and there wasn't anything they could do. The chance of her surviving was 0.1 percent.

They couldn't find her lungs, her heart wasn't formed well, her superior vena cava wasn't there, and her Aorta was very small. They said she could grow fine in my womb, but when she was out, they would not have a way to save her. They asked if I wanted to keep her and I said yes. I heard her heartbeat. I didn't have the courage to end her life.

When I got home, I called my mother. She completely disagreed with my decision. She said I should take that baby out now. Taking care of a disabled child is not easy. She reminded me that I had already seen the difficulty with my sister and her disabled child. As a mother, how could I just agree to stop the heartbeat? When Joe and I decided to keep her, until she arrived, I went to the hospital every two weeks. I spent three to five hours there and that became my routine. I got so exhausted with all of the different examinations I had to go through every day.

The bigger she got, the longer I had to stay at our appointment. I truly believe God could do a miracle, but me and Joe were not at the same level of faith. I told the church what was happening, and the pastor and elders came together to pray for us. They continued to pray for two weeks. I remember having this dream where I was climbing a mountain. I had my first child on my back and I was pregnant with our second child. In order for me to climb that mountain and get to the top of the mountain, Joe had to push me. He couldn't in the dream. He was too weak. He could not push me to get on top of that mountain.

As soon as I woke up, I heard God's voice so clearly. He said, "I am sorry." I knew right then, right there, that because we did not have enough faith in our house, God couldn't do anything about it. Since I was a kid, God always talked to me in dreams, or showed me things to come in my life. I never took my dreams seriously. I learned a valuable lesson, without faith, God can't do anything in our life. We are the one blocking our blessings.

I wasn't mad. I knew I was carrying a dead body in me. She would kick and play. I sometimes woke up in the middle of the night in a panic. I knew that she was not going to be with us. It was so stressful all of the time. I trusted God, but this was too much for me. On May 10th around 4:00 PM, I was sitting in the living room. I got up to go to the bathroom, and when I came back and sat down my water broke. Joe called 911. I could not believe the amount of fluid that came out of my body at that moment. It felt like it was over ten gallons of water.

We arrived at the nearest hospital around 2:00 AM. When she came out, she was silent and did not cry or make any noise. I was crying out to God. I just wanted to hear her cry, but nothing happened. She was quiet. I was in so much pain. Yet, I forgot about my pain. She was so beautiful. Square face, just like me, she was a big baby.

The nurse checked her heart and there was a weak beat. She asked me if I wanted them to do something to save her. I declined. The nurse kept checking her every five minutes, and forty-five minutes later her heart stopped beating. She was gone. I cried. Not because she was gone. I cried because of the memories we created together.

We had fun. We went to Walmart together. We went to school together. We worked together. Showered together. Talked, and walked in the park. We had wonderful memories together. She was supposed to be my Princess. She helped me finish high school. When I didn't feel like doing my homework, she kicked me. We had so much fun together. Now in five hours, she left me for good. They took her to the funeral home.

On May 15th, we arranged her burial. We went to the Funeral Home and picked out clothes and everything for her. Church members organized everything for us. The song was beautiful and comforting. Our Pastor, Sheldon Bryant, gave the best ceremony, and Elder Richard gave the best testimony.

When they were lowering her down into the earth, it was raining. No one minded getting wet. People were full of joy. I had peace letting her go.

If your relationship stresses you, I hope you will find the courage to recognize it and put an end to it. Don't be like me and regret the ten years spent in a relationship that didn't serve me. Don't spend that much time invested in something that you know will not work for you.

This is the spirit of a warrior; follow your heart.

65

This is dried meat cooked with peanut butter; Dek Ari Mopwo

Chicken is very important in our culture, we call it Dek Gweno, in Acholi, and we eat it for any occasion, especially at celebrations.

When the new bride goes to her husband's house, she is first given chicken. The bride must know how to cut the chicken into 12 pieces. Then the elders will count it.

Blackeyed peas cooked and served with shea butter oil on top. We call it Dek Ngor, and it is also an important traditional meal cooked in celebration of a newborn.

Raw sesame butter cooked with dry meat. We call it Dek Lamimo
or Lakokoto

This unique food in our culture is not easy to cook. We ground the
raw sesame, and after grounding it in a tray, it is processed to get
the oil out. We do this by timely adding small amounts of water to
get the perfect texture. You have to be patient when cooking this.
The amount of water must be just right.

This is cooked vegetables with peanut butter. We call it Dek Aguru, in Acholi. This is another one of our important dishes. It looks simple, and many other tribes make this dish, but we have our own special way of cooking it. It does not taste the same!

This is yam; we call it Layata or Liyatat in Acholi. It tastes like sweet potatoes, except this is textured.

This is roasted sesame butter. We call it Odii in Acholi.

This is Millet Fufu. We call it Keon Kal in Acholi. This grain is one
the best health grains in the world. You can find it in African and
some Indian stores.

This is Blackeyed peas bean leaf. We call it Dek Boo, in Acholi. We eat this plant from leaf to seed. This plant is easy to grow. In America, we grow it every summer.

This is called Awal in Acholi. We use this for many things; carrying water, a cup for drinking, serving food, or an umbrella for the newborn baby. It is also used as a musical instrument.

This is still culturally accepted, and we continue to use it today in our tribe.

This pot is called Agulu. It is a cookware that is past on from generation to generation.

Culturally, dancing has been an important part of the Acholi people; entire communities incorporate dance as part of their rituals and celebrations. Besides the actual dancing, clothing and other adornments, such as anklet bells, and beaded necklaces, plus musical instruments, become an important part of the dance.

This machine is used to ground the grain; we call it Kidk Acholi.

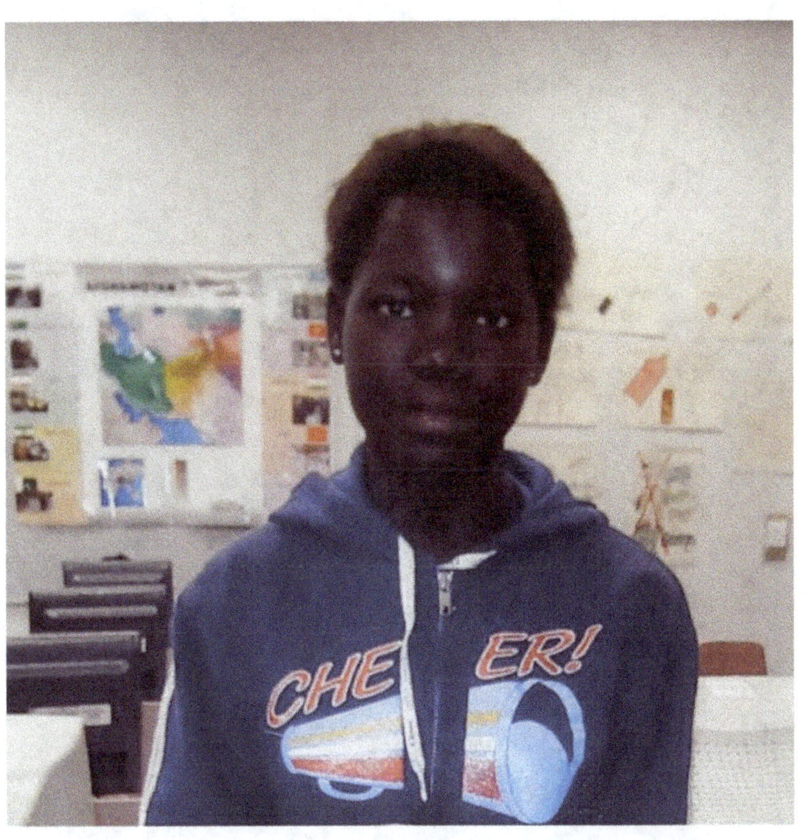

First day of school in America.

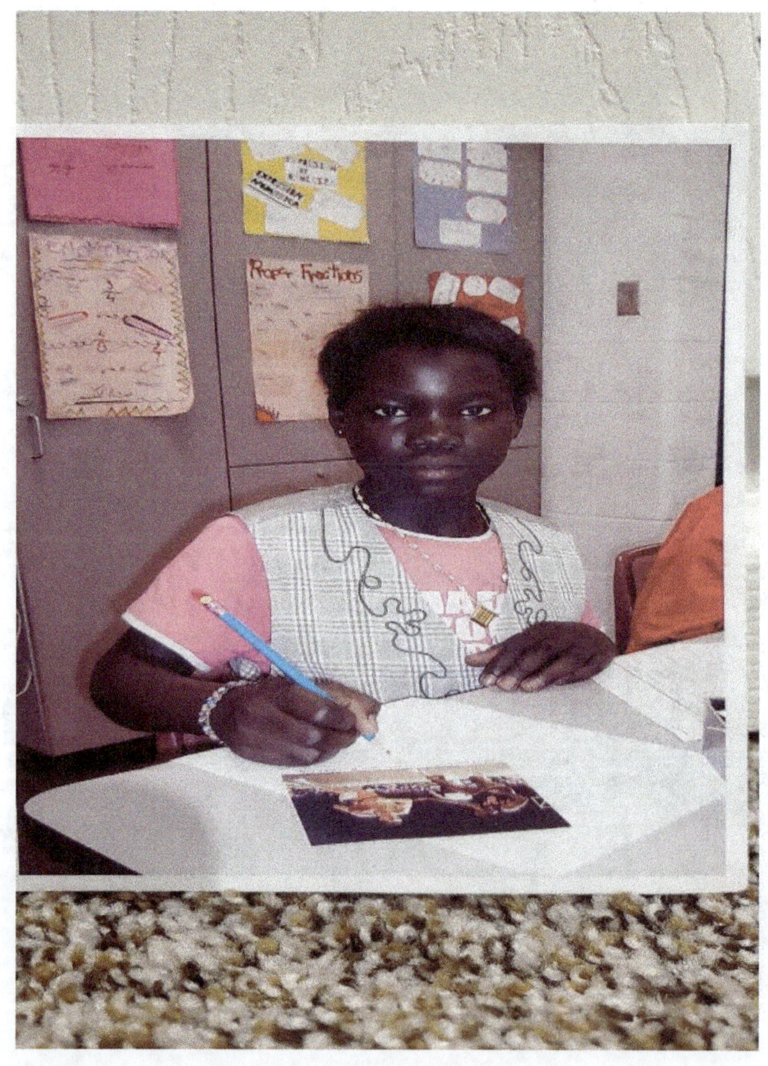

First day in my history class.

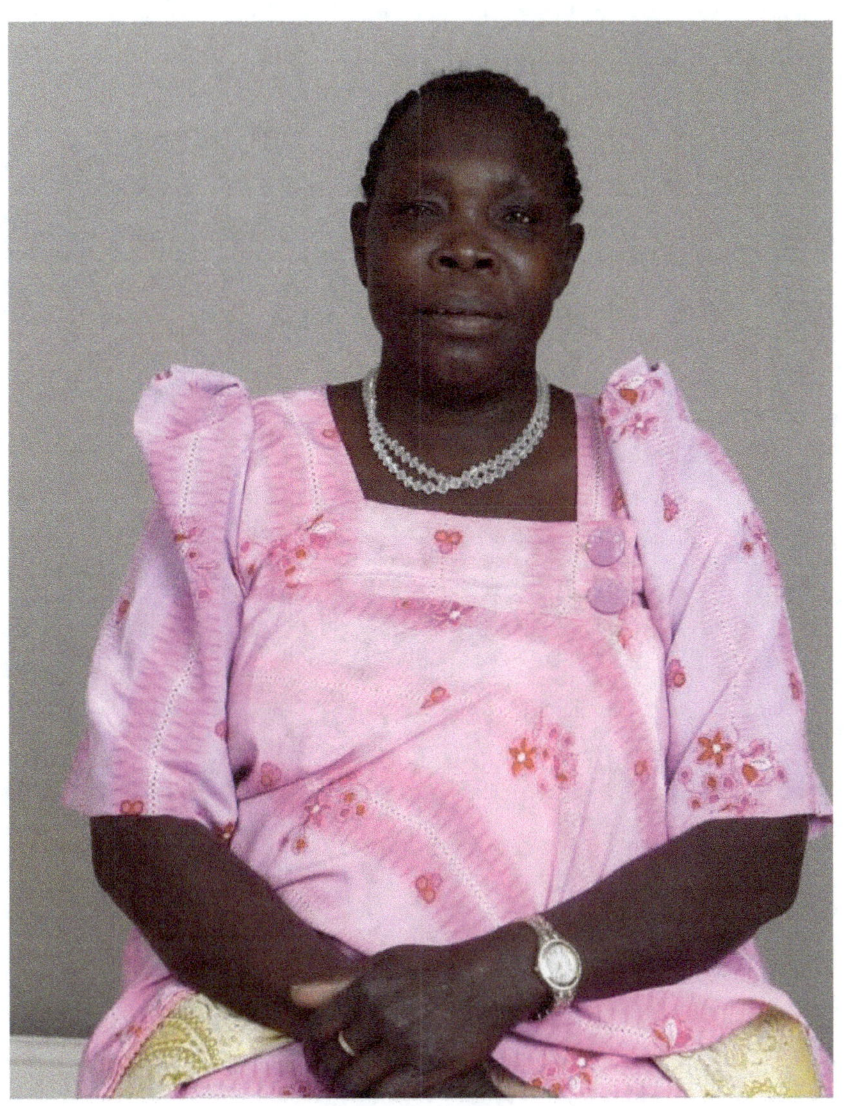

My beautiful, strong mom.

Me and my four boys.

Family

CHAPTER FIFTEEN

Pregnant Again

After my daughter died, I knew I had to get out of the house. I went to Idaho two months after my mom came to visit us and left. I told my mom I wanted to go back home. This relationship was not going to work and I knew it. I wanted to get out and start fresh in life. We packed everything for my son and I. Joe drove us to Idaho, and I didn't tell him we were done, but in my heart I knew it was over.

We had sex to say goodbye and two weeks later, I found myself in the same position. This time I was mad at God. I didn't understand God's creation. Why did He give me another baby? One I could not take care of. I got a job at Wendy's that I did not like but I was committed to doing what it takes. Five months into the pregnancy, my feet hurt and I couldn't work. Living with my mom was not an option. My mom was nice, but sharing a house with her was a problem. She already had stress in her own life. I didn't have a choice but to go back to Utah.

At the time that was the only option that came to mind. Instead of looking for assistance, and until I could stand on my own feet. I had learned that the relationship was not going to work. People think when you have a baby you are automatically a mother or a father. It doesn't work that way. Fatherhood is a learned experience. Not everyone who has children is a mother or father. We have babies everywhere, but there aren't many fathers! The definition of Father in English is very weak. Father is a source, the foundation of the family.

If you can't treat your wife like a human being, you have no right to be a father. If the roots of a tree are rotten, how can it bear good fruits? I was staying in that relationship because of my paradigm. The programming of my brain was too weak to understand myself. I couldn't understand why I kept going in circles. Until I started to change my mind about programming. I didn't know why I was listening to the pastor preaching and reading the Bible. I was listening to a book, and started asking questions of myself.

What am I doing with this man? *Habits are God's way of making good automatic in our gift* – Robert Russell. I didn't form good habits when I was young. Somehow, I knew I had to change my way of thinking to be great.

The Spirit of Warriors: Never stop learning. It will do you good.

CHAPTER SIXTEEN

Moving To Iowa

I thought changing locations might do something good in our relationship. To be honest, I wasn't changing the location for our relationship. I was searching for myself. I knew there was more in life than just fighting. I was done fighting. I wanted to find myself and live the life I saw in my imagination. I saw having a good man who would care for me. I wanted to own a business, live in my dream house, and drive my dream car. I always wanted more in life.

I didn't want to see it on television, I wanted to live it. I always questioned myself. How are those people on television different from me? I spent two to three hours sitting on the couch watching them. Most of the time the television was watching me! Halfway through the movies, my brain would be in action. If I was watching Oprah, soon Oprah would be interviewing me.

Moving to Iowa reprogrammed me. After moving to Iowa, I was curious to be more. I had to pick myself up and get on with it. Do it all over again, only even better this time - Sam Walton. I went back to Walmart, but not because I liked it. I went back because it felt like it was a safe place for me. My first job in America was at Walmart and I loved it. The people were nice and they appreciated me. My boss told me I did a good job, and the customers appreciated how fast I was.

When I married Joe, I didn't feel safe anymore. I wanted to feel safe again. I wanted to feel valuable, and important. When I went back to Walmart a second time, I was getting good feedback. I worked my way from the backroom to the front-end Manager. I saw everything and I was incharge of everything. Yet, I still felt something was missing.

Our store manager was a woman named Shannon. She was very smart and a strong woman. Everyone thought she was mean. I liked Shannon, because she was a no nonsense woman. I wanted to be like her, walking with confidence and having my own Walmart. That didn't last long. Five years at Walmart was enough for me.

"God's gift to you is more talent and ability than you will ever use in one lifetime. Your gift to God is to develop and utilize as much of that talent and ability as you can, in this lifetime." - Steve Bow

Going back to Walmart was my comfort zone. I had to learn to get out of my comfort zone and know that it's ok to make mistakes. Having four kids was not going to stop me. When I finally broke my paradigm, everything started to make sense. I knew then, the location would not change a man. I learned that a man who refuses to change, can't be changed. I could not change him.

I figured I could change my environment. I owned the power for my happiness. Not Walmart or moving to Iowa. I could start to love Iowa and make something out of my life. So, I did just that. I quit Walmart and started to build my own territory within me.

The Spirit of Warriors: Work on yourself before helping anyone. You can't gift what you do not have.

CHAPTER SEVENTEEN

Healing

I was a year old when I got a disease on my right shoulder. The disease killed a lot of people, both adults and children. Since I was only a year old, I believed it was not my time to go. I thought the same as when I was nine years old. I was lying down and really sick. I heard my mom call my brother and ask him to call Grandma. She said your sister will not make it tonight.

I was weak and didn't have any more strength. I was coughing and coughing all day. My cough began when I was probably one or two weeks old. When my mom was pregnant with me, there were so many bombings. Although she wasn't smoking, she inhaled all the pollution, smoke, and chemicals in the air. These things affected my lungs.

I remember when I was seven years old and my mom took me to the doctor. They couldn't figure out what was wrong with me. They put me on this medication and I had to have ten shots. One per week for ten weeks. Going to the hospital became my routine. As I was lying on my deathbed, mom did something amazing. As soon as she told my brother to go and call grandma, she picked up a hand-made broom to sweep the front of the hut. She wasn't praying, but challenging God. She asked God a question. She said, "If you did not want her to stay with us, why are you letting her suffer this long?" I did not know who God was at the time. Deep inside of my heart, I asked God the same question.

I didn't really know what it meant to pray and I was never taught how to pray. I remember when I was about five years old, my mom gathered us together in front of my hut on a Sunday morning. Before she went to work in the garden, we sang one or two worship songs, and she would pray. Then they left us at home, her and my older sisters would go to the garden. My job was to take care of my siblings, but I loved going to church.

I would follow our neighbors and wear the small dress I had with a hole in it. One day, I remember one bishop said that God doesn't care about the way we dress. He only cares about our hearts. At five years old, I had a pure heart for God. I didn't have shoes, and the weather was hot, but I would run from tree to tree for the shadow to cool me down on the way home.

When I heard mom ask God the question, I asked God the same question, I felt the healing go through me. I started to gain some energy. My eyes opened. I saw the sunshine again. I didn't know much, but I got up the next morning and I was fine. God healed me.

Spending ten years in a relationship was not so bad since I was young. I was twenty-six by the time I left, and maturing. I knew right and wrong fully now. Science explains brain development and suggests that most people don't reach full maturity until age twenty-five according to npr. com. It helped me to heal from all of the pain. I would wonder what was wrong with me, because I knew from the first day of the marriage that it was not going to work.

I kept going back and forth, but I knew who my husband was. When I talked to James, he made me feel so good and at peace. He would ask me why I didn't leave Joe and focus on my school and why do I have to wait this long? The ten years that I wasted in the marriage, I could have been a doctor. I was blaming myself for not seeing this earlier in the relationship.

I don't remember everything about my dad, but mom told us stories about how bad dad was with her. When she would tell the stories, her face and mood changed completely. I can see her pain through her body language. She hated my dad so deeply. As a kid, I didn't like to see my mom this way. She was a strong and hard-working woman. She blamed her father for not putting her in school. She always said, "If my father put me in school, I could have been the president of South Sudan. Those men in the leadership positions, didn't know what they were doing."

My mother was naturally a leader. She did not need to go to school for it. She raised eight children by herself. She knew how important education was for us. She gave up her husband and came to America so we could be educated. Mom really loved my stepfather. He was a wonderful man. I learned from him what a good man should be. He took care of my mother well.

I heard them at around 4 AM in the morning talking. There is nothing more beautiful than hearing a man wake up in the morning and make plans with his wife or just talk. Our elders always said the problems in marriage are fixed in the dawn before birds start their praise. The four men I had in my life helped me to know what I wanted in life.

My father was dreadful to my mother, but my stepfather was gold from heaven. He took care of my mother and cared for us as though we were his own children. My Ex-husband was dreadful to me, and my lovely husband now, was sent into my life from heaven. Sometimes we have to go through horrendous experiences in life, but that shouldn't define our future. I have turned all of my pain into helping people.

Since I was always a sick child, I didn't really have any friends. I had to learn to identify people's personalities and understand why they acted the way they did. I learned how I could counsel them, because I had been in their shoes. Growing up in a refugee camp helped me to understand the life of a refugee. I also learned how I can be the bridge between refugees and those who have never been a refugee.

Getting pregnant and being kicked out of the house at a young age helped me to understand child brides. This was a big problem in the world with children being forced into marriage against their will. Living in an abusive relationship, helped me to value my marriage and help women going through bad relationships. I taught them confidence and how to find themselves in life.

We all go through something in life. My experiences gave me a PhD worth of experience in life. I speak with confidence about it too. I have no shame. It was the school of life. The education is higher than what you get from the classroom. With classroom education, everyone must take the same class to graduate from school. However, I am the only one who can understand and speak about the trauma I went through.

As I sit in my office across the street from the Iowa governor, tears of joy come down my face. If I didn't go through a bad marriage, I would not have thought about starting a company to bring flexible hours for families. Instead, I probably could have gotten my University degree and lived comfortably elsewhere, minding my business.

I don't blame my past experience. I love my past. I don't try to get rid of my memories. I love them, because they remind me to keep going, but they have no control over my life. My memories and my past are in the back of my car or in the backyard. When I am home, I can't allow them in our home, because their feet are too messy. I permit them to cheer for my future because they like to brag about being the birth of my future.

Why should I blame them, everything must start somewhere right?

The Spirit of Warriors: Persevere. Hard times don't last.

CHAPTER EIGHTEEN

Getting Off Of Housing Assistance

The Housing Act was established in 1937 to help families get a decent home and a place to stay when they need help. Government assistance housing is really to help people who need it, but there are so many people taking advantage of those programs. They can work and live the American dream, but they choose not to because they know the government assistance is there for them.

I lived on government assistance for nine months. I hated every single part of it. I did not like to depend on the government. I had to struggle to live my life the way I wanted to live it. During my time on assistance, I knew of people who just didn't want to work. Others I have seen in the refugee community. America does not have strong systems in place before bringing people to America.

The system introduces people to free living and after the benefits are gone, there's no system to help people to live their full potential. There are ESL classes, but Africans are hard working people and very smart. When they can learn how to get certified training in a specific field, or learn how to run a business smoothly, they could help the community.

So many businesses failed because people got in trouble with taxes, and didn't know where to go to get help. My business is running because I had a friend, Michelle Bartusek, who helped me. I met Michelle when I took a class with the Iowa Center for Economic Success. She was a beautiful woman inside and out. She was there with me all the way. When I wanted to get my LLC and EIN number, she did that all for me.

She became part of my business. She helped me in many ways. When I had questions about sales tax, withdrawing, and other questions, she helped. When the pandemic hit in 2020, Michelle lost her job with the Economic Center, but she never left me. She continued doing my taxes, and when I started to hire workers, she was there helping me. Now she has her own business doing taxes and payroll.

She was one of those beautiful souls in my community. She didn't care much about how much money I had to pay her. She just wanted to see the world as a better place, and I was grateful to have her in my life. For those who are refugees in America, when we come across someone like Michelle, who guides us through the system, we don't struggle as much, because of their guidance.

However, we have to be willing to find someone like Michelle. We can't just sit and hope someone will show up and give us what we want. It is not easy for people to pay an entire rental payment, and have a full time job when they sit at home watching TV and eating all day.

I wish the American system was a little bit better in those areas. I wish they looked at the history of a person, and assess whether they could work. If they couldn't work, why couldn't they work? If they are healthy human beings, why do they have to be on government assistance? The American system is great, but when it comes to understanding who needs help and who doesn't, it is not so great. I think ninety percent of all of the Africans who come here are healthy. They can work and they can make their life better if America were to have a better system to train these people.

When they get to this country, the system could start training them on their mindset. If you can do more and be more in this country, you don't have to live on housing assistance and depend on welfare for food. There are many areas where America can improve to be an even better place.

Most Africans go through trauma and obstacles that put a boldness in us. We may not know where to go, where to start, or how to live life at first, but if somebody guided us from the time of arrival to America, we could be so much better off. There are so many African women and men with talents. Their talents are all at a meat factory or some other factory. They end up going to work at factories, and they don't like the job, but they have to work to support their families.

There was no strong foundation to find their talent or to put them where they belong. All they know is that they are in a new country and they must go to work. I wish they began working on refugee's mindset instead of trying to find them job skills or handing them assistance. We saw the same thing happening in 2022 with Afghanistan refugees. They are in Iowa and some of them don't have a place to stay.

I read one of Elizabeth Warren's books where she talked about how the White House looked like a White House, but they are completely divided into Republicans and Democrats. They are not working to help all the people, they are looking out for themselves and their party's interests. Instead of finding out what is best for human beings and how they can serve.

If we all worked together to find the solutions for the immigrants or refugees we bring into America, it would make a big difference.

My friend Caryn and I came together to open a career pathway to help refugees. We are a bridge between refugees and American citizens. We help them to understand what it means for refugees to come into this country. We also help American citizens to understand and recognize their new neighbors. Those of us who've been in this country for twenty years plus. We help them so they understand how we can come up with a much better system so we can make the world a better place.

Living on housing assistance for nine months opened my eyes to see the needs of the community. The need is greater than what we can see. My heart is truly to help the people who are suffering right here in our neighborhoods.

There are so many young men and women in jail, because there's not a strong enough system to help. There is no organization that targets the needs of the young people to help change their minds.

We could all make America a great place to live if we took the time to understand, and helped the youth find their full potential so they can prosper in life. Rather than living our lives in a small house and never thinking about our neighbors. Maybe we do think about them, but we are not contributing to their mindset.

When most people get to America, people are handing them fish. People are not teaching them how to find a good river, showing them where the fish is coming from, or how they can learn how to fish for themselves to support their families.

The Spirit of Warriors: Learn how to live independently!

CHAPTER NINETEEN

Habitat

In 2013, Habitat accepted us. I was so excited! In the Habitat program, you had to be willing to donate 400 hours of your time before they would build your house. You could do 200 hours, and that put you on the list to find a place. We did everything we could. Every weekend we were busy building a house for the people that already had a place.

In the Summer of 2013, we were offered a place to build our first home. It was fast. I manifested our home. I drove around Des Moines, looking at those beautiful homes and imagining myself owning one. I truly believe in the power of imagination. In the Spring of 2014, we started to build our home.

In August 2014, we closed on our house. It was built by Habitat for Humanity (Habitat). I hated living in this housing. Every single day I drove around and prayed. I was hoping that I would own a house. I wanted to live in a house with a backyard. I liked seeing my kids playing outside. I worked really hard, and I was doing everything I could to find a place for us.

On August 19th, we finally got the opportunity to witness the dedication of our home. On August 26th, 2014, we closed on that house. We could finally move in. We did not bring anything from our house, because there were bedbugs and cockroaches everywhere. We only brought some cookware. They gave us this savings account. They matched every dollar we put in.

All together we saved $4,000.00, and as promised, they matched it, and we had $8,000.00 at our closing. That helped us live in the home for one year without paying a mortgage. It was so helpful! This led me to look into going back to school, or starting a training program. I began training at Project Iowa and it opened my eyes to the possibility of finding myself.

The Spirit of Warriors: Be willing to manifest your imagination into your reality.

CHAPTER TWENTY

Baptism

After we moved to our new house, I ordered a cable network that had 3ABN, the Hope Channel, and Amazing Fact TV. It was all Adventist services. Our home was very religious. All we watched on TV was religious programs. I grew up catholic. We ate whatever and dressed however.

Joe knew that I was Catholic and he thought he could change me to be whatever he wanted. I remember hearing him talk with one of his relatives. The person said, "I heard you married a young girl. That is good. You can train her in the way you want her to be." I looked at Joe's face, and he was happy about it. He tried to change me for the last ten years we were together.

He said I could no longer wear makeup or braid my hair. I could not wear earrings, or high heels. I dressed like a person in my fifties. I didn't even know who I was anymore. I loved watching Tyler Perry movies. He said I could no longer watch that. I could not eat bacon and sausage, because we were Adventists. Don't get me wrong, I am still an Adventist, and I don't eat bacon or pork.

I am a vegetarian most of the time, unless I go to a farm and see the animals that I am going to eat. Otherwise, I don't really eat a lot of meat. I did choose to convert to Adventists, because I liked the way they taught the bible most of the time. Also, I didn't want my kids to go to two different churches, but we had a lot of fights about clothes and food.

Joe was expecting me to just change into this Adventist woman, who would dress and behave a certain way without formal training. I have loved going to church since I was a little girl. I went to church for me, not for other people, but Joe made me hate going to church with him. We looked so perfect as a family, but we fought from home all the way to the parking lot.

After Joe got out of the car, his attitude completely changed. He personified a happy man. I hate to pretend in life. It took me eight years to finally decide on my own to get baptized. I thought to myself, if Adventists live like Joe, I can't become one of them. It took me listening to the Adventist home book by Ellen G. White, the co-founder of the Seventh-Day Adventist Church to decide to accept the Adventist fate.

I asked him, did you read the Adventist home book? He said he did.

I thought to myself, I shouldn't even say a word. This book was full of information on the family and how a Christian home should be. The book taught how a man should treat their wife and how wives should treat their husbands. It showed how a family is a little heaven on earth. I shouldn't have continued with the conversation. I knew this man would never change.

A few weeks after I was watching 3ABN, Kenneth Cox came on, and he was talking about baptism. The way he explained it made sense to me. Right then, I decided to give my life to Christ and get baptized. Pastor Jeremiah scheduled my baptism.

I woke up that morning and prayed to God. I asked him to give me a miracle and take away my memories. I didn't want to remember Joe. When I came out of the water. I heard God in a different way. I had my own will, and I had my right to choose my own way. I put myself into certain situations. God didn't put me in the relationship with Joe.

God warned me before I entered the relationship. It was my choice to choose what is best for me. When I walked out of the water, I felt the power of confidence. The more I got closer to God, the more distance came between me and Joe. Some grow together in a relationship, but others grow apart from one another. We grew apart. The more knowledge I got, the less we had in common.

He chose not to change and there was nothing I could do. I knew it was just a matter of time. Sometimes we try to do things in our own way, but God's time is not our time. It took me another two years to make my decision. One thing about me is that I learn, and learning has been my way out of any situation. For the LORD gave wisdom; from His mouth comes knowledge and understanding. Proverbs 2:6.

I never questioned God's love for me. I do sometimes question Him in private. He is our Father. I can't talk about my family business in public, but we all have times where we cry in our bathroom, rooms, or car. It's a special time with the Father. I never said that God did not care about me in public. I knew deep in my heart that He does. I am a beloved daughter of the King, and I stand by my words.

The Spirit of Warriors: Know that you are worthy.

CHAPTER TWENTY ONE

Development Class

I call Tony Wilson the father of Project Iowa. Tony is a father to many women and men who go through Project Iowa training. Project Iowa is a job training program. They do more than job training, they provide self-development too. Every time someone told Tony their story, he'd close his eyes and listen. Once they were done, Tony would always say something meaningful.

I recall sharing my story with Tony. I saw him close his eyes and when he opened them, the first thing he said to me was, "You're a fighter." This is not the first time I heard this word to describe me, but the way he said it to me stuck with me. Tony was about four feet in height, light-skinned, African-American, and he was about fifty years old. I felt like he was a father permitting me to be myself. Two weeks into the class, I asked one of the counselors a question about relationships and self-confidence. Mr. Duc said, "Lily, imagine you get into a fight with someone, and they cuss you out, and tell you that you are like an octopus, and you have eight legs." Do you believe them when they say you have eight legs, or should you let it go, because you know you do not have eight legs? I said, "I shouldn't believe them, because I don't have eight legs, I have two."

He said, "Exactly, but imagine, the same people keep repeating the same words to you. Would you believe you have eight legs and start acting like an Octopus?" I was quiet. He said, "Exactly. Now your brain is in confusion mode. The more you keep hearing bad things about yourself from people you think love you, the more you will start to believe it. Learn how to believe in yourself."

I have learned so much from this program. I learned how to set goals. Both personal goals and professional goals. Looking through my notes, one goal that I have been writing since 2014 is that I want my kids to grow up in a good environment.

The Spirit of Warriors: It's ok to let go.

CHAPTER TWENTY TWO

My Spirit Troubled Me

I remember when my mom gathered us together for worship on Sunday morning. We'd sing one or two songs, and mom prayed. She was a single mother raising eight children. She didn't have time to go to church, but she always made sure we prayed. I grew up knowing how to pray. I didn't know much about the bible, but I knew God was real. When I met my Ex, he was an Adventist and as we started going to church together, I started to learn more about the word of God. It took me about eight years to really understand a bit about God.

In 2013, I started to question my beliefs and challenge God. I told God I wanted to know more about Him, and I wanted to live the happy life that He promised me. The more I searched for God, the more He revealed Himself to me. Jesus Christ talked about helpers He would send, to guide us. I didn't know what this meant. How can I get the help that I need from the Holy Spirit?

I misunderstood the message. Looking back, the Holy Spirit tried to warn me. Then the Holy Spirit did everything He could to get me out of the situations I got myself in. It was very clear. When I was dating Joe, me and the Holy Spirit got disconnected.

I didn't listen. In 2010, when I lost my daughter, everything in my soul told me to leave, but I didn't listen.

The Holy Spirit is the spirit that lives in us. The spirit who guides us. The spirit who shows us the way to live. The spirit who screams out when we're doing something wrong. He will tell us in the still small voice not to do something, but most of the time we don't listen to that small voice in us. Our body is the temple of the Holy Spirit (1 Corinthian 6:19). The Holy Spirit is a very important being in our lives.

Genesis 1:26 says, then God said, let Us make man in Our image, according to Our likeness, let them have dominion over the fish of the sea, over the birds of the air, and over the cattle, over all the Earth and over every creeping thing that creeps on the earth. Father, Son, and Holy Spirit, separated themselves from us, because we lost our rights to the dominion. When Jesus brought the dominion back to us, as in John 10:10. He knew we needed help because we are still living in a sinful world.

John 14:16 says, I will pray to the Father, and He will give you another Helper, that He may abide with you forever. God is a king. Jesus is our attorney, a lawyer standing on our behalf, and the spirit is our mediator. He will take our issues back and forth to our Father God to guide us, and help us in any decision we make. Most of the time we pray to God. We cry out to God. We cry out in Jesus' name, and we forget about the spirit that is in us. That is the mediator between us and God.

When I finally learned how the Spirit worked, I couldn't live with Joe anymore. My spirit was not connected with Joe. Some people go to church, but the spirit they have in them is not a good spirit. When you have the Holy Spirit in you, and when you listen to your Holy Spirit, as soon as you meet someone, you know whether they have a good Spirit or not. I won't say my Ex had a bad Spirit. I don't know what it is, but it was not matching with my spirit anymore. I got the message that I must get out now and that God would take care of me. I listened to that message.

Whatever decision you make, listen to your heart. If you have peace in your heart, know that it's a good thing for you. If you don't have peace making the decision, question yourself and pray more about it. As soon as I started listening to my spirit, more doors opened for me. Now, I live a life where day by day, before making any decision, before going into any business, before I decide on anything, I always ask my spirit to lead me. He always leads me in the right direction.

God promised that He would never fail us. God sent me in this world to do something important. I believe strongly in my heart that everybody is special. Everybody has a gift and everybody is here in this world to do something great. It's up to you to take the time to find out what God sent you in this world to accomplish. How can you find out the gift He sent you here for? Jeremiah 29:11 says, for I know the plans I have for you, declares the LORD, plans to prosper you and not harm you, plans to give you hope and a future.

If you can just take your time to listen to your spirit, it is a beautiful thing. Since I discovered this, I have never stressed out. I never worry about things, because I know that all things work out for the good, for those who trust the Lord. I believe that I have found my calling when I work to help the refugees here in America. It doesn't feel like work for me. I feel good. More and more, the idea kept coming to me. So if God can do that for me, I believe God can do this for you too. Spend time in the word, and pray more to find out who you are.

The Spirit of Warriors: Always listen to your intuition.

CHAPTER TWENTY THREE

Jail

In 2017, I finally made up my mind that I could no longer live how I was living. I decided to move out of the house that Joe and I bought through Habitat. I tried to kick him out of the house. Joe will not give you mercy. If he can kill you, he will. I saw the house was not worth my life. I decided to move out. We'd been going back and forth for almost six months.

In April of 2017, I moved out and went to live with my mom in a two bedroom apartment with my four boys. That was a bad move. I worked full time, and I could afford a two bedroom apartment, but I didn't think of that at the time. Then people started talking. In America, a woman does not leave the house. The man leaves. People told me to go back to the house and kick him out.

I had to remember the reason I left the house. I left the house because I knew this man was dangerous. I was afraid for my life. My family knew he was a bad man, but they didn't know him deeply enough. I knew Joe, but I still listened to people and went back. We talked, and he decided he would move out of the house so I could live in the house with the kids. However, that was not what he did. When I moved back in, he thought we were back together. I didn't share the room with him, because we were 100% done. Some men do not know the meaning of, "I am done with you!" It means nothing to them. If a woman says she is done, she has had enough of everything. She means there is no more forgiveness. He didn't want to leave the room.

I made myself a place to sleep in our unfinished basement. My friend suggested this. My friend said it's good for parents to stay in the same house for the sake of the kids, if you two can understand each other. I have learned that this depends. If you are able to then maybe you can, but if not, please don't try to do things for kids. Those kids are better off with you two leaving each other, rather than having two crazy adults who become enemies to each other. The kids will become victims of the problem.

I thought we were no longer a couple. We were roommates. So I was talking with James. Of course, I shouldn't have done this.

We started sharing pictures with each other. One day, I put my phone on the table. Joe grabbed my phone and ran into the car. He started going through my messages and found everything he was looking for. Private messages to James. Things he was looking for to prove I was the bad person. I didn't feel guilty about it, because we were no longer sharing a bed.

When the elder came, he told them all of those things. I agreed with everything. I didn't hide who I was, or what I had done or said. In that moment, Joe became the innocent one. In my community, when there are problems in marriage, two families come together to solve the problem. As a couple, you are to share your problems, and elders are the judges. We do not go to divorce court.

I was very honest with them. I appreciated them coming, but when I was done, they insisted that we fix our problems. I declined and told them ten years was enough. I was proud of myself for saying that. Most of the time in our communities, women do not have a voice, until others see the man is about to kill the woman. Then they give her the information she would need to leave the relationship.

It is too late for some of the women who are physically abused. After the elder spoke, we decided I would go back to our bedroom, and Joe would sleep in the other room. Joe stopped the physical abuse in 2013, because I warned him that if he even put his hand on me again, I would call the police. He stopped putting his hands on me, but mentally he was seriously abusing me every day.

The power of words is worse than someone hitting you physically. I didn't want to die young because of the relationship. After we had another fight about the phone, he took my phone again. It was a Galaxy S8. A brand new phone that was $800.00. The phone would just be taken from me, just like that. I was so mad I tracked the phone. He took the phone from our home and went to the Community College. From the Community College, he went to his cousin's home, and from his cousin's house to Grayslake.

I assumed he threw the phone into the water, and that is why the tracking ended. I asked him, but he refused and denied taking the phone. In Joe's mind, he thought my phone was the problem. I was working overnight cleaning, so I dropped the kids off at my mom's house and went to work. When I got out of work, I went to the house to get the kid's clothes for school. I found him sleeping on the bed I was sleeping on.

I asked him what he was doing. He said, "This is my house. I can sleep anywhere I want to sleep. We talked back and forth, and things heated up quickly. He got out of the bed and came toward me. I already knew this was not going to end well. He tried to hit me and I grabbed him. We fell on top of the laundry basket and the basket broke. It scattered everywhere. The basket cut him more than it cut me, because he fell on it.

I fell on top of him while he was in the basket. We wrestled and I got loose and ran outside. I didn't have a phone to call the police. I ran to the neighbor's house to borrow their phone, but it was already too late. Joe already called the police. When 911 asked what his emergency was, he reported, " My wife came home this morning and while I was sleeping, she tried to kill me."

I'd been in America for twelve years. I had very few interactions with the police during that time. I was once stopped by police because while working at FedEx, I would start at two in the morning without any sleep at all and I got pulled over. I'm glad I did because it looked like I fell asleep while driving and the police said I was driving 100 mph on the highway.

After Joe called the police, they came to the house. I didn't know how to talk to them. I was nervous and it was cold outside. From my body movements, according to police training, they thought I was lying. They believed Joe. What Joe said was true, but it was also not true. I did not try to kill him. I wanted to get my kids clothes and wanted to live in peace.

It was ten years ago, on June 19th, when I walked into Joe's room. I remember there was a cold breeze in the room. I knew something was not right, but nobody taught me how to listen to my heart. At the time, I didn't know what else to do. I thought the best thing to do was to stay. Now ten years later, I am walking away in handcuffs. I went to Joe's apartment with his car, and I left in the police car.

This is something I avoided for him. I never wanted to cause Joe to be arrested. Despite him breaking my nose and blackening my eye. I would blame it on my son when they would ask me at work. I'd be lying to the doctor when they asked me whether I felt safe at home. This is how Joe betrayed me. He lied to the police by saying that I tried to kill him while he was sleeping. I walked with a knife to try to kill him. Really? Me!? I gave him four beautiful kids. He couldn't at least respect that? All I tried to do in our relationship was protect Joe from the criminal system. I didn't want my kids to have a father who went to jail. Well now, they had a mother who went to jail.

Still, I thank God it was me. If Joe was the one to go to jail, I would have felt bad. Joe, on the other hand, put a restraining order on me to stay away from him. This helped me to come to my senses. I finally saw myself and my identity. I saw the Queen that I was born to be in this world. It wasn't easy. Even though I released myself from him, I fell into depression. Not because I missed him, but I was mad at myself for not listening to my heart.

I was mad at myself because I kept having children. I was mad at myself for not being me. I started to take five to six Ibuprofen to get myself to sleep. I was going through the pain of regret. I wanted to numb myself from the pain. I wanted to be okay. One thing I continued to do, even though I was a mess, was keep listening to Les Brown, Joel Osteen, Jim Rohn, and other motivational speakers.

I knew what I was doing was not okay. I needed help, but I didn't know where to go. Life and business are like the changing seasons: You cannot change the seasons, but you can change yourself. There's an opportunity to live an extraordinary life. The opportunity to change yourself - Jim Rohn.

I knew I couldn't take back the ten years. It's gone. I must forgive myself and move on with life. Now, I am free to prove Joe wrong. All of the lies he told me. I am not stupid. I am worth more than a ruby. I am beautiful. I am wonderfully made. I was young and immature, but now I am grown. I have owned my powers. "Once social change begins, it cannot be reversed. You cannot uneducate the person who has learned to read. You cannot humiliate the person who feels pride. You cannot oppress the people who are not afraid anymore." – Cesar Chavez. I have found myself within.

Our Own place

After three months of living with my mom, we moved into our own place. My two oldest sons were not with me yet. Joe and I were still in a custody battle, and Joe didn't want me to get the kids. He took me to court again and claimed he was afraid of me, and needed a restraining order. My lawyer was there with me, and he was excited because we won.

For me, it was a waste of time, because there was already a restraining order in place.

I'm not sure what he was scared about, but whatever it was, it did not make sense to me. The judge asked him why he thought he needed a restraining order, and asked what I did? All he could say was, "She's a bad woman." He told the Judge that I loved men when we were living together and that I would bring men into the house when he was not there. He said that one day he came home and found a condom in our backyard. Everybody in the courtroom was confused by what he was saying.

What does finding a condom in your backyard have to do with you being scared of your wife? I thought that was kind of stupid, but people can be stupid. They just dismissed all of the claims he tried to allege. The custody battle continued. Finally, on November 17, 2018, I got custody of all the kids. We finally brought them home.

When we moved into our town home, I did not have any money to buy furniture. The church donated a bed for the two youngest sons, and a friend from my network group donated a bed for the two oldest.

I was sleeping on the floor while still trying to find my way out. Our divorce was ugly. He was disrespectful to my family and my mom. In my culture, that brings a curse to the children we have. No matter what the situation is, you're to show respect to the in-laws. Joe went to my mom's house to grab the children with the police the morning I got arrested. My mom did not agree for the kids to go with him. Then he called my mom "This Woman," which is an insult in my culture. He then told the police that this woman tried to kill him.

The police weren't sure what was going on, but they had to do what they had to do, because the kids were his. the disrespect, he showed my mother, I would never go back into Joe's house. There we were, living in our three bedroom townhome. It was affordable for me. In my heart, I knew I wanted to own a home and live the American dream. I knew I had to keep praying, and working hard on my business so it could grow.

My cleaning business began to help both my family and those in the community. When we cleaned people's home and they had things like furniture, clothes, cookware, or any other useful thing, they donated it to us and we would give it to people in need just like I was. Since I had been in that situation, I wanted to help people going through it. I found myself owning a cleaning company, but it was not enough for me. I was looking for something greater than me.

On October 20, 2020, I worked all day. When I came home the kids were making noise as always. I sat down at my dining table. I lived in a small, three bedroom townhome with my four wonderful boys. We had a kitchen, dining room, and living room all together. In under 300 feet, we had cockroaches climbing on the wall. I was feeling so disgusted and I prayed to God every day, asking for a new place.

I had a cleaning business, but the business was running me. I was busy crying out for God, but God was waiting for me to take the first step. While I was sitting at that table, I didn't feel like eating anymore. I grabbed my phone as we always do and went on Facebook. For over five years, I listened to Les Brown and followed him on Facebook. They started Power Voice in June 2020, and I ignored him. Yet, that night, he posted a video of himself dancing. I thought that was funny. Uncle Les can dance.

There was something different about that video. I went to bed, but I couldn't sleep. Around 11 PM, I heard a clear voice asking me if that was all I saw. That got my attention and I messaged the Power Voice team. I didn't commit right away. It took me two days, because I was still asking God for a sign. Finally, on October 22, 2020, I signed up.

All of my life, I compared myself with Jonah in the bible. When God said go right, I went left. Until life turned on me, then I moved. I learned the hard way. Do not be like me, because we are all sent into this world to do something great. God didn't create you to just exist in this world. There's something here for you to accomplish and if you don't do it, someone will suffer in life because you decided to keep quiet.

Our world can be a better place if we all did our best in life. Dr. Myles Munroe gave us five questions every human being must answer. Whether a man living under the bridge, a millionaire flying in a private jet, a politician running for the White House, or church leader leading a church. We're all struggling with his five questions. These five questions are controlling the world. The questions are as follows:

1. WHO AM I? IDENTITY
2. WHERE AM I FROM? HERITAGE
3. WHY AM I HERE? PURPOSE
4. WHAT CAN I DO? POTENTIAL
5. WHERE AM I GOING? DESTINY

What is God's will for your life? God's will for your life is for you to die empty; leaving this world fulfilled as Jesus did on the cross, and say "It is Finished." As Apostle Paul said, "I have fought the good fight, I have run the race, I have kept the faith." As women, we already have those in history who fought for us. Now is our time to pick up the baton and keep on the race. We have to be stronger than ever before, because we have the knowledge, wisdom and understanding.

The Spirit of Warriors: We keep fighting no matter what.

HOME AGAIN

Owning a home in America is the American dream. Since I came to this country in 2005, I heard some people saying they would never own a home in America. I wondered why. In reality, in order to live the American dream of owning a home, you had to make an investment. Owning a home was part of the investment. I loved those beautiful big mansion houses. Every time I cleaned and walked through them, I imagined living in one.

When I moved to Iowa all I wanted to do was own a home. That's why I went through Habitat. I was trying to do everything I could to become a homeowner. That is one of my dreams I had when I moved to this country. When we got the Habitat house, walking out was heartbreaking, but it led me to own a better home.

After leaving the Habitat house, and living in my mom's two bedroom apartment for three months, we finally found ourselves in a townhome. This was closer to the neighborhood with beautiful houses. Every time I drove by I always had this image in my mind that I wanted to live in those beautiful houses.

The first year of my business, I made $36,000. In the second year, I made $70,000, and in the third year about $140, 000. I employed about six employees by then. I am grateful for them, and I continued working hard. I had already found myself and I knew exactly what I wanted to do.

I learned that the American dream belongs to those who work hard. In January, 2021, I finally called my brother William. He was a Realtor. I found William back in 2019. He was one of those brothers who loves you unconditionally and does anything to help. I told him I needed a house and he was there for me. He went on his own way to find us a home.

There was a house in Pleasant Hill that went on the market the same day. Right away, he called me and I made an appointment to go and see the house. As soon as I walked into the house, I took a deep breath and said, this is my house. He said, "You love?" and I said, "Yes!" I sent out messages in every group asking for prayer.

We put in the offer, and I hoped they would accept it. They put the house on the market in the morning, and we put in the offer in the evening. My offer was accepted the next day! Everything was done by April 12th with closing. We blessed the house on the 14th, and we moved in on April 15th.

I am an Ambassador in this world and my home is the embassy of heaven, so it should be seen from far away. That is exactly what God gave me. I know that whatever you want in this world, you will get it, but it comes with a price. I believe it all starts with imagination, dreams, and clear vision. It starts by writing things down and believing in your imagination. I always have a vision board. I got exactly what was on my vision board.

The Spirit of Warriors: Believe in your imagination.

CHAPTER TWENTY FOUR

My Love

In November of 2012, I got a friend request on Facebook from Langoya James. I looked at the screen and my whole body went numb. This can't be! Was this my James? I thought to myself, opened my Facebook and clicked on the picture. Yes! There he was. I couldn't wait to get out of work and just look at the picture. I didn't even have to talk to him. I just wanted to look at the picture.

James found me in 2010, but because of poor connection in Africa, we lost contact. I received his friend request and that was an amazing feeling. I can't ever describe it. I got out of work and sat in a parking lot for two hours. just looking at his picture. I loved James and I knew he loved me too.

When we were in Africa, I never felt well. I was always sick and was always alone. I didn't have any friends. I would take care of the animals we had and they were my friends. When James moved to the camp from South Sudan in 1999, we became so close. Every time he came back from school, he started teaching me about the things they learned. He also told me about his story from South Sudan, and shared how they left, and came to Uganda.

I grew up in Uganda, and didn't know a lot about South Sudan. He told me about his mother, and how he lost her when he was one year old. His mother's friend took care of him, and came with him to Uganda. He became a true friend to me. He wanted to see me happy. I am not saying this because he is my husband now. He really cared for me at a young age. I loved the way he made me feel. Maya Angelou said that people will forget what you said, people will forget what you did, but people will never forget how you made them feel. I have learned this.

 In the year 2000, we were old enough to work for mangos. We usually went to work in someone's garden, and they paid us with mangos. It was a fun thing for us kids. We were living in a refugee camp and working for Ugandans citizens who had a lot of mangos. One day, I carried wood to trade for mangos. I was the only one who carried the wood, and this family accepted my offer.

I had to be left alone because the others had to go on to find work. It was about seven of us. James was among the seven and he said, "I will stay here with you. I can't leave you alone." We went and started collecting mangos. We had a lot of fun climbing mango trees. We ran around the mango trees.

I don't remember all that he said to me. When we were there, I claimed the tree and peed from the tree. He said my pee dribbled on him. Oh gosh! I don't remember that, but I remembered the safety he offered to me. I don't know what would have happened if I had to go home by myself from ten miles away. We didn't bring home many mangos, because we ate most of them. We didn't get home until 5 PM.

He always loved me unconditionally. It wasn't even about me being in America. He loved me when I was in Africa. He loved me when I was playing alone with the animals. He helped me when I got so sick, everyone was afraid to sit close to me. He comforted me at the time I needed it the most.

In 2000, we moved out of that neighborhood. Someone sold us their plot when they left for America, but their sister wanted the plot back. It brought conflict between our family and theirs, and this led to us losing our little sister. Her name was Stella. My mom had Stella with my stepfather. Stella was just like me. I loved her so very much. She was smart, beautiful, and bold. We looked alike.

When I started school, she always waited for me by the road. When she saw us coming home, she ran to us and grabbed my plastic bag that I carried my books in. She was smart. I blamed myself for a long time for my sister's death. When she started school, my mom asked me if I could bring her home on my break every day. I agreed. After a month, I thought she had friends she could walk home with. Just that one day, someone poisoned her. The next day, she started getting sick. Within a week, she passed away. I was so hurt.

I always thought, if I had just dropped her home, she might not have been poisoned. It took me a long time, until 2018, to forgive myself. I had to tell myself if that was God's will, there is nothing I could have done differently.

Moving to our new place was not by choice. Our house was not finished yet, but we had to start living there in our unfinished hut because when my sister passed, we couldn't stay anymore. James moved to a different place too. I didn't know where, but he was going to a different school. We started seeing each other again in 2003. When he moved to live with his auntie, our schools were in the opposite direction.

We used the same road and I would see him sometimes. In 2004, he started to send his friend to let me know he wanted to talk to me. I rejected the offer, then he asked my friend if she could let me know that he wanted to talk to me. I rejected that too. He never gave up. He kept on bothering my friend, until she begged me to go talk to James so he could leave her alone. I agreed.

We were the professional traditional dancers when there was a community gathering. After the dance, we finally met behind the school building. I remember sitting on the classroom window. I was thirteen at the time, and James was seventeen.

He came and met with me. We only talked for five minutes. Soon, we heard some of the other girls, my friends, on their way to collect water as well. We decided to stop talking. I ran into the bushes to hide and he went down the road, and just took off running. I ran into this drying bush that sticks on your clothes and hair. Since it was dry, I got it all over my hair and clothes. We laugh about it now.

We hid our love life and kept it a secret. I didn't talk to him again until January of 2005 when our name came out.

One thing I remember from that night was that he held me so tight he could feel my breathing and my heartbeat.

I'd been with my Ex-husband for ten years. I did date some men in between our divorce. Finally, I came to my senses and realized that James was the one. Nobody held me tightly the way he did back in 2005.

We reconnected in 2010, and I didn't talk much. I was married at the time. Our communication was on and off until 2016, when my Ex and I were living like roommates. We started talking more, and the love grew. The next thing I knew we were sending inappropriate pictures to one another. This was a bad idea. I should have left my Ex first.

In 2021, I told my sister I was going to Africa to meet with a man I've been talking with for the last sixteen years. She didn't believe me. She said, how can that be? How can a man and woman be apart for sixteen years and the man waits for the woman? I got the ticket in 2019 because I wanted to go, but everything was shut down. The plane was shut down and the country was locked down because of COVID. I couldn't go until August 2021.

I finally made up my mind that I wanted to go to Uganda, and see this man with my own eyes. On August 3rd, I left the country and went to Uganda. My flight took three to four days because of COVID. We landed on August 6th and were finally face to face. I was sitting on the bed. He was sitting on the chair. We just looked at each other. We couldn't even say a word. It seemed impossible. I couldn't believe it. I was sitting in front of this man I've been talking to for the last eleven years.

It was the most beautiful thing I ever experienced.

I was deep in sleep. When I woke up at 2:00 AM, I was hearing him pray. He was kneeling down right beside the bed, and he was thanking God for finally bringing us together. God just woke me right at that moment to witness a miracle right in front of me. The man of my dreams. Someone with the same faith as me. My heart was full of joy. I lay with tears of joy in my eyes.

We spent two weeks together. One week at his house. I had peace with James. That's when I knew it was true love. I watched movies about true love, but I had never experienced it in real life. That's when we decided to get married. It was before I came back to America. I didn't go to get married. I wanted to meet him. We talked with Bishop David Otto on August 18th. My flight was leaving on the 26th. We only had five days, but this church came together and planned everything in three days.

On Monday, August 23, 2021, we got married. We broke a record in Kitgum. Nobody gets married on Monday. Everything went according to plan. This time nobody was forcing me to get married. I was following my intuition. All of my family thought I was crazy. They thought I lost my mind. They did everything to stop me. My mom and dad gave their blessing, and that was all I needed.

Everything was beautiful. I married my best friend. He was my best friend since we were kids. We made a promise under the mango tree twenty-one years ago. Our words came to pass. Sometimes we keep asking God for what he already gave us. If we took the time to listen to Him, and listen to our heart, everything we need would be right there in front of us. It's up to us to open our eyes and our mind to see.

If I had accepted James in 2010, when he reminded me about our promise, I could have saved myself from a lot of pain. Still, I'm grateful that I went through the pain. I went through the training to know how to love a man and how to identify a good man. Living with my Ex-husband and going through all of the obstacles I went through, it was training. When the time came for James and I to be together, I knew what it meant to be a wife.

I know what it means to support a man or myself, and I know what it means to love a man. I know what it means for a man to support a woman and stand by her. We will be the strong couple that God wanted us to be. Whatever we go through in life, if we can turn it into a learning lesson and never go back or never repeat mistakes, we will get something out of it. We will learn something beautiful from it.

There are still some good men out there. Don't let your past experiences stop you from loving again. Turn your pain into a lesson learned. Never look at your pain as something that will destroy you. Always find a lesson in it and live by knowledge and wisdom. This will manifest all the good in your life.

The Spirit of Warriors: Never underestimate your words.

CHAPTER TWENTY FIVE

Fasting

It was May 2017, when I decided to do an Esther fast. I was already doing some fasting, and I was doing it once a week sometimes. I wasn't serious about it then. In May, I took some time off from work and fasted for three days and three nights. After my fast, I couldn't sit still anymore. It was like something woke up in me. I started focusing on my health, exercising three times a week, and I went vegan. I didn't eat any animal products and I lost about forty pounds in one year. Things became more clear to me.

Even though I was going through the divorce and other obstacles, I was strong in my faith. In 2018, I went back to Project Iowa and talked with Julie. I wanted to start a nonprofit organization. I wanted to help people and I needed more help with my ideas. I had already started Cleaning for Hope in April of 2018. I was doing the cleaning by myself at the time, but I felt like I could still do more to help people.

Julie connected me with Caryn Kelly. She was a woman I called my twin sister from a different race. Caryn was a beautiful Caucasian woman, in her forties at the time. We were both going through a divorce. She had two handsome boys and she had a heart to help humanity and all races. After graduating from college, she went to Mexico for a year. After that, she worked at the Arizona border for seven years. Meeting with Caryn helped me to understand my purpose in life.

We met at my house and talked for about an hour. She was in the process of buying a cleaning company for the same cause I stood for. She was creating jobs to help refugee women in America. We became like sisters. She introduced me to Patty, another beautiful Caucasian woman. Patty owned a cleaning business for fifteen years. She was skinny with blonde hair and had a beautiful soul. She was a strong believer in God. Patty introduced me to twenty-one days of fasting and prayer.

I never heard of such a thing before. I grew up hearing that if you go three days without food you will die. Here this woman was, talking about twenty-one days of fasting. She bought us a book by Jentezen Franklin on fasting. I read the book before January of 2019, and I decided to do twenty-one days of no food and just water. I started on January 5th for the entire month. After twenty-one days, I didn't feel like eating anymore. It was such a wonderful feeling. My whole body was changed.

I was back to my normal weight for the first time in the fourteen years since I had been in America. I didn't do it to lose weight, but getting back to my regular weight was amazing! So was the power I gained from the fast. I remembered all of the dreams I was having. It was God's promise to me. My future was very clear. It led me to meet Kaitlyn Huiseberg, a salon owner. She wanted me to clean her house. She was a wonderful woman with determination in her heart. She took me to her network group, and this was an open door for me.

When I started my business, I didn't know anything about networking. Business Networking intentional (BNI) was the best thing that ever happened to me. I thank Kaitlyn for that. As I continued with my journey to success, I decided to make fasting a part of my life. We, as believers and Kingdom ambassadors, must fast and pray to continue the work strongly. Jesus said in Matthew 6:16, "When you fast, do not look somber as the hypocrites do, for they disfigure their face to show others they are fasting. Truly I tell you they have received their reward in full."

Through my experience, I would recommend fasting for anyone who is willing to make some changes in their life. If you have some health issues, I recommend seeing a professional first. Fasting is a time set apart to seek the face of God. It means abstaining from other things that you find pleasure in. The process is to give your whole heart to God in prayer. When you fast, you are telling God that the prayer and answer you are seeking are more important than the pleasure of eating.

Fasting means putting God first. You are to focus all of your attention on him alone, and not on his gifts or blessings. Just focusing on God Himself. It shows God how much you love and appreciate him. Fasting is a point of intimacy with God. God will reveal Himself only to the people who want to know him. He says you will seek me and find me when you seek me with all of your heart (Jeremiah 29:13).

All the greatest Saints in the Bible fasted. David, Abraham, Moses, Jeremiah, Daniel, Anna, Paul, Peter, Esther, and even Jesus himself fasted. Fasting is one of the pillars of the Christian faith. It is mentioned in scripture one-third as much as prayer.

It's important we understand fasting. I recommend you grab some books on fasting. Here are some scriptures to help you: Joel 2:28-29, Acts 2:16-18, Isaiah 58:6-9,11. You can also use Google and YouTube to help you understand more about fasting.

The Spirit of Warriors: Understand your rights in God's Kingdom.

CHAPTER TWENTY SIX

Whatever You Lock on Earth will be Locked in Heaven

I never understood the meaning of this message until March of 2022. I was sitting in our house, alone and hopeless. Well, maybe I had a little bit of faith. I was hoping God would come through, because I needed Him more than ever now. Sometimes people say they need God more than ever in life, and you don't understand what they mean, until you go through the experience. Finally, your eyes open to the knowledge and now you know.

I was off that day because we only had two houses to clean. I sent two of my workers and called one to tell her to stay at home. We didn't have enough work. It had been three months now and we were barely making the bill payment. In February I took a trip that I couldn't afford and went to Africa anyway. I was following my heart. Then, I was in trouble, deep trouble! I couldn't breathe when I started thinking about it.

Payroll was due on Friday, and it was Tuesday. I had hundreds of dollars in the business accounts and my personal account was negative fifty-six dollars. Five hundred were coming from Venmo, and I had about four houses to clean before Thursday. There was money that customers owed me in the amount of about two thousand dollars. I needed about six thousand and two hundred dollars to cover the payroll, and my mortgage was due on the first of the month.

Last month, I already borrowed two thousand five hundred dollars from my mom, so I'm thinking, now what? What can I do? I thought, I do have some friends. Maybe I can reach out. They could help me from the deep hole I put myself in. Yet, I didn't want to borrow money anymore. I was tired of borrowing money. I was tired of having financial problems. I was tired of crying to God. I was tired. I was tired. "Where are you when I need you!? What have I done so wrong in this world that I am trying my best, and you are not helping me? What is it that my ancestors have done that the curse keeps following me? Why, why, why Lord?" As I burst out in tears, I blamed myself. I should not have taken that trip to Africa. Maybe I should stop following my heart. Then what? I heard myself and I sounded so stupid. Then I wiped my tears and trusted God. I told myself that with the little faith I had, I had two more-days and God could do a miracle. I believed and hoped.

Early that morning, when I woke up, I heard that voice. It came to me. Whatever you locked up on the earth, will be locked in heaven. As I look back on my life, for the last six months, I wasn't so faithful with my tithes. It's not because I didn't want to, but because I was questioning the church and the teaching in the church. Now, I wondered why? Because church is church. Church and Christianity are different. Church is where people come together, church will never change, no matter what you say or do.

My question should have been, why do I go to church? Why do I pay tithes? Am I doing it unto men or unto God? Now I am sitting here and crying out to God and wondering why I am not crying in church. Malachi 3:10 says to bring all the tithes into the storehouse, that there may be food in my house says the LORD of host. If I will not open for you the windows of heaven and pour out for you such a blessing that there will not be room enough to receive it. This is what every church preaches, but it has nothing to do with money.

You have to read this book (the Bible) from the beginning to the end if you still don't understand it, read it in different versions and if you still don't understand it, please listen to the audio version. If you speak different languages, they have the Bible app in many different languages. Knowledge is the key to life. If you don't understand something, you will not get it right until you understand it. It's good to pay your tithes, but was God only talking about money in Malachi? Or was He referring to how good a covenant with God is, and our lifestyle to our fellow humankind?

The Spirit of Warriors: Get wisdom, knowledge, and understanding.

PRAYERS

What is prayer? And why do we pray?

Of all the things Jesus' disciples observed Him say and do, the Bible records that they asked Him to teach them how to pray. Luke 11:1 Now it came to pass, as He was praying in a certain place, when he ceased, that one of His disciples said to Him, "Lord teach us to pray, as John also taught his disciples." As I sat there on Friday, with my bank account at negative $1,700, I was wondering what I did wrong. What should I have done differently? Is my prayer not effective? Of all the miracles Jesus has done, why did they ask Him to teach them how to pray? Can't we just talk to God like normal people the way church teaches us, or does prayer need to be learned? Jesus did answer him in Luke 11:2, so Jesus said to them, "When you pray, "Say..."

The Model Prayer

Before we get into the model prayer the church teaches us, which is the Lord's Prayer, consider why the bible says this is the model of prayer? We see the words "model" in many things. I think of a car model, phone model, appliances model, and so on.

Here are definitions of the term Model:

1. A three-dimensional representation of a person or thing of a proposed structure, typically on a smaller scale than the original.

2. A system or thing used as an example to follow or imitate.

Did you get the two words in the definition of a model? Structure and system?

Structure: the arrangement of and relation between the parts or elements of something complex.

System: a set of things working together as parts of a mechanism or an interconnecting network.

Many of you love to learn new things like me. Now you know that the Lord's Prayer is not all about repeating what is in the Bible without learning how to pray. Many of us grow up in the church and call ourselves Christian. Yet, the model prayer has nothing to do with going to church, or repeatedly saying the same thing over and over. You can't hope somehow something magical will work in your life. The model prayer needs to be taught in class. The church was supposed to be that class room, but we are all so broken in the church. We need a new group. Les Brown said, "Only Quality People (OQP)." I am not saying to get out of the church, but surround yourself with positive, like-minded, people who are willing to learn, and want to understand what the good book says, and own your power!

Jesus said in Luke 11:2-4, When you pray, say

"Our Father in heaven,

Hallowed be Your name

Your kingdom come.

On earth, as it is in heaven,

Your will be done on

earth as it is in heaven.

Give us day by day our daily bread.

And forgive us our sins,

For we also forgive everyone who is indebted to us.

And do not lead us into temptation,

But deliver us from the evil one."

The prayer looks so simple and easy to remember, but it's not. The disciples lived with Jesus. They went everywhere He went and observed Him for three and a half years. Still, based on the Scriptures, they still asked him to teach them. We can deduct that Christ prayed for approximately four to five hours every morning. He also prayed at other times. It is very important for us to realize that regardless of the name it has been given, what Jesus explained to His disciples is not really the "Lord's Prayer." It's a model for prayer. In other words, you don't need to repeat the words of this prayer exactly. Instead, you can use them as a pattern to fulfill this purpose. In doing so, He gave them this model to follow.

OUR FATHER: Our Father the first thing we learn is that we are never to bring only ourselves in prayer when we approach God. We ought to bring other people's concerns with us. Most of us go to prayer with our own shopping lists, we ought to think of others as well as ourselves.

IN HEAVEN: When you pray, remember that you are not praying to someone on earth. Why? Because that is where the problem is. You need external help when you say our father in heaven. You're saying to God, I recognize that I need help from the outside.

HALLOWED BE YOUR NAME: The word hallowed means reverenced, set apart, or sanctified. This means he is the Holy one. There is no other like Him. Hallowed be His name. Then Moses said to God, "if I come to the people of Israel and said to them, The God of your father has sent me to you,' and they asked me what is his name?' what shall I say to them? 14 God said to Moses, "I AM WHO I AM." He said, "say this to the people of Israel, I AM has sent me to you (Exodus 3:13-14 RSVCE). His name is holy, and He is not what you want Him to be in your life. At the moment you need Him, repeating the model without identifying your need for God will not get you anywhere.

1. Jehovah -Yahweh: I AM WHO I AM (Exodus 3:14)

2. Jehovah-Jireh: Our provider (Genesis 22:14)

3. Jehovah -Raphe: Our Healer (Exodus 15:26)

4. Jehovah -M-Kaddesh: Our Sanctifier (Leviticus 20:7-8)

5. Jehovah-Nissi: Our Banner (Exodus 17:15)

6. Jehovah -Shalom: Our peace (Judges 6:24)

7. Jehovah- Rohi: Our Shepherd (Psalm 23)

8. Jehovah-T'sid-kenu: Our Righteousness (Jeremiah 23:5-6)

9. Jehovah -Shammah: Our Faithful Companion (Ezekiel 48:35)

There are thousands of names for God in the Bible. Do not limit yourself into repeating what is already been said. Be creative with God. He is Alpha and Omega.

YOUR KINGDOM COME; YOUR WILL BE DONE: This statement simply means that a true person of prayer is not interested in his own Kingdom. His interests are in God's Kingdom, and what he wants to accomplish. We should always ask for the fulfillment of God's prayer list before our own. This is the reverse of how we usually do things. We are to ask the Father what He wants done? Because we alone will not know what we were sent into this world to do. The list from the father is a clear way for us. We are all sent at different times and for different needs. What Esther did back then might be the same thing we deal with now, but we will need to go in different directions to accomplish it. For example, if I want to help the refugees in America, fasting and going to the President might not be an option.

GIVE US OUR DAILY BREAD: In Jesus' day, the term "daily bread" was a cultural idiom that referred to everything necessary for the making of bread. Therefore, when you say give us our Daily Bread, you are not only praying for food, but also for the whole process that is necessary to make the food possible. If we pray this, we are asking for the soil, seed, sunshine, nitrogen, oxygen, nutrients, minerals, time, growth, development, harvesting and everything the farmer needs to produce food. We're thanking Him for this store where we're getting the food from and bringing it home. Whatever process the food went through, we ask for blessings to clean out any chemicals, so we can put healthy food in our bodies.We also want to put others in our prayer, as we are thankful to get food to eat. We are thinking about those who don't have any food around the world.

FORGIVE US OUR SINS, FOR WE ALSO FORGIVE: Jesus is dealing with relationships. He is saying your prayer has to take into consideration those with whom you are in a relationship. When you come before God, check to see if anyone has anything against you, or if you are holding anything against anybody. Don't come into God's presence and expect to have your prayer answered if you are asking God to forgive you, but you are refusing to forgive others. Sometimes, we have to look into ourselves and check if we have forgiven. We can't allow the person to hurt us. Praying that God forgives us our sins is not all about what we have done wrong. It's about what we hold onto, and have not allowed ourselves to not get healed from. Praying that God forgives us is asking us to go deep within ourselves.

DO NOT LEAD US INTO TEMPTATION: This does not mean that God might steer us toward temptation against our will. It means that we are to ask God for wisdom so we won't put ourselves into a situation that will cause us to compromise our relationship with Him. In other words, we are to ask God for strength and wisdom to stop making bad decisions, and to stop going into bad situations that will tempt us to sin.

YOURS IS THE KINGDOM, POWER, AND GLORY FOREVER: After you have prayed, then worship the father again. When you do so, you are saying to God, I know you are going to answer my prayer. Therefore, I am going to say thanks ahead of time. I am going to give you all the glory that comes from what happens. When the answer is manifested, I am going to tell everybody that it is because of you. All the power and all the glory belongs to God forever.

I sat in my house and began to understand all of this. My heart was at peace. It flows like a river from the Mountain top. Knowledge is the key to life. Solving the problem didn't happen overnight. I was looking at the problem in different ways. When I went to Africa with my friend Simon, to open his school, it opened my eyes. This gave me more knowledge on what to do. When I spoke at the Lopalo school to all those girls, and saw their reactions, it gave me hope to continue doing great work in this world. Sometimes, we must go through tribulations to understand our purpose and keep going. Success is not an easy road, but with much knowledge, it will be easy. I did work my way out of the debt and continue running my business strong

The Spirit of Warriors: Understand your WHY.

CHAPTER TWENTY SEVEN

Transformation

When I look over all of my life, there was a pattern in my life in April, August, and November. These were important months for me. I began my period in April of 2005. I started the ninth grade, and began learning my ABC's in August. I had my first child in November. I left my relationship with Joe in April. I started a business in April. I went back to Africa in August. I published my first Anthology in November.

When I started to identify those little things in my life, I began to understand my superpower. It's not about my lovely husband, it's not about my beautiful children, it was all about me. I had come to my senses. I searched for myself. I started a business, but that still was not it. I love what I do. I love helping women. I bought a house with a big garden. I love our home. I spoke at a school in Africa, and helped those girls build confidence. I got a new office for my business in a place I love. In all I have done, I found one thing. I have to live life for ME. Just one word is so important: Transformation.

We don't find it in something else, but from within. I was my barrier in everything I went through. At the end of the day, I had a choice to make. Should I continue dwelling on my past, or should I share my story? This is who I was. I love writing. When I wrote, I felt like myself. I didn't have to be Oprah Winfrey, Viola Davis, or Angela Bassett to share my story. My story was about me.

I love those women dearly. I keep my heart close to them. When life gets too tough, those women are my reminders that If they can continue to climb the mountain, so can I. Even if they lose strength I can continue on with the strength I have gleaned from them. We all have different paths to follow, but we all look for the superpower the creator put in us. Whether you are born in a refugee camp, in a poor or nice place, with both of your parent's love or not, we all have one thing in common. We all want to be loved and to be knowledgeable about what we do.

The world will be a much better place if we can learn how to love each other. For God so loved the world, He gave His only begotten son, that whoever believes in Him should not perish but have everlasting life. Love!

We can't seem to go within ourselves to find that Love. A man beats his wife because he didn't have love as a child. A mother screams at her child, because she didn't get love as a child. The world is fighting for power, killing millions of innocent people, and other countries, wanting to own more power and kill for love. At the end of the day, it doesn't matter how powerful you are. All you want is for someone to love you.

If you can stand with confidence and tell yourself, "I love me no matter what," we would not have the courage to hurt other people. When your heart is filled with love in overflow, you will have enough to share with the world.

The Spirit of Warriors: Learn how to love yourself first. Then you will have enough to share with those around you.

CHAPTER TWENTY EIGHT

Management

Use your time wisely - Nelson Mandela

When I look back on the time I wasted, I realize it was over thousands of hours. I was just working. I'd come home, cook, eat, fight, and sleep, every day for ten years. I didn't think of reading a book, or learning something from YouTube to improve my life. I was depressed and living the life I didn't want. There's one thing in life I have learned. It's not about your family or who you married. It's not about your location. If you are not living your purpose, you will be depressed.

We are all created with the power to live to our full potential. God himself wasn't satisfied in Genesis 2:5. Before any plants of the field were on the earth and before any herb of the field had grown. For the LORD God had not caused it to rain on the earth, and there was no man to till the ground. God had put His power in us. We want a good life, a beautiful family, nice house, nice car, and good kids, but we don't want to put in the work. In the NIV translation, to "till" means to work. There was not anyone to work the ground, and so God caused nothing to grow. How can we grow in our life, if we don't put the time in?

A principle on why we are here in this world is found in Genesis 2:5-19. For me, the Bible appears to be the instruction and constitution of God's

Kingdom sent down on earth. It's not a religious book. We didn't lose heaven. We lost earth, and as long as we think we are not from earth, we can not solve the world's problems. Earth got nothing with all of the pain we are going through. We human beings created our own constitution that we proudly remember, and we seem to be happy with it.

I am African, and that doesn't match where I have gone into the world. Africa remains in me. Americans went to Africa and brought the people to America as slaves. They did everything they could to take Africa out of those they took. That was four hundred years ago. Yet, African-American's still love collard greens with cornbread. It doesn't matter where I am in the world. I will still need my collards with fufu. That's what makes me who I am. I will have a hard time in heaven if God does not plan on having fufu in heaven. If we can start to think about the earth as where we belong, the world would be a much better place. We would allow Jesus to come back, and he would know that we are not desperate to leave earth.

Look at it this way. Everything from Genesis to Revelation is all about the coming of Jesus to save us. It reminds me of going from slavery to having refugees coming to America. God is trying to tell us something. God made America like a small heaven. Everyone in the world, it doesn't matter how good their country is, they are all desperate to come to America. America sounds like Heaven. If you are living in a different country, it's difficult to come to America. If you make it, thank God!

However, you still have to work hard to make it in this country. You might say, well heaven is different. Why did God allow colonization in Africa? You might say, heaven is where we belong, and if not, why are we going there for thousands of years? Revelation 20-21, says we are the ones holding the second coming of Jesus. If we can learn how to live like Kingdom citizens, we will have no problem going there. Someone said, imagine God taking you to Heaven with the mindset you have? You would start digging the gold from heaven's roads. We have our own power within us. We can start living in peace now, and start by managing ourselves.

Five years ago, I learned about not worrying about my tomorrow. It sounds crazy, but I never had a single day of worry in my life. I was in South Sudan on August 16, 2021, and we were about to leave on the 17th. For some reason, we didn't because we were waiting for James' brother. On the morning of the 18th, when we were ready to leave, we heard there was an attack on the road and five people were killed. People were worried, but I prayed and had in my heart that God would not bring me this far and allow death before I complete my mission.

I learned how to conquer my fears. Anyone on earth can do it. You cannot overcome and live the Kingdom life, if you don't want to manage yourself and leave your fears and consequences out of your territory. God wants you to enjoy life now. Heaven will be like coming to America when your country is at war. When your country has peace again, you will be eager to go back. Managing our lives well and influencing the next generation will give us hope.

The Spirit of Warriors: Take full control of your life.

CHAPTER TWENTY NINE

Queen

I remember the day like it was yesterday. The weather was warming up and we were going through a divorce. I wanted my Ex to move out, but he resisted. I was done with the relationship ten years earlier. It was time for me to leave the relationship, but I was still feeling bad for him. Even though I didn't want to live with him anymore. We had been together for ten long years. I became accustomed to the bad life. While I was crying out to God and wanting to change my life, I couldn't seem to move on. Then God had to move on me. When God moved, I listened.

It was painful. I was sitting out that day, and questioning myself. Who am I in this world? Why am I here? I wanted to know. I heard God loud and clear. You are Queen Lilian. You may wonder why I have chosen to share my story right now. My answer is, why not now? So many of us are too ashamed to share our stories. We think about whether we didn't finish school, or think we are not good at spelling the words out. We think about those things because we are from refugee camps.

I read the book *Becoming*, by Michelle Obama. In the book, she said we can't wait for the world to be equal. We have to become equal with the world. We all have a job to do. We cannot wait for the world to be equal, the world will never be equal. Even the Bible shows the world is not equal. After the Garden of Eden, Adam and Eve lost their power. Even after Jesus Christ came and died on the cross, and brought the power back to us, we still have problems.

If only we understood that power. If we knew how we could use that power we could become the people we were created to be. I recommend you watch the documentary *Becoming*, with Michelle Obama. I also recommend the Oprah Winfrey and Viola Davis film, and Beyoncé's homecoming. These are powerful women, who remind us of the power in our lives. You can watch the Mary J Blige documentary. Steve Harvey has a great book called *Act Like a Success, Think Like a Success*. When you don't have much knowledge, you can listen to or read those books.

You feel their stories, but you never look through it and say can I be one of them? Why not be one of them? They don't have any kind of superpowers in them. All they have is a little bit of faith to keep going. Even in times where they felt the darkest, and most fearful, they didn't quit. I have learned not to quit no matter what. I ready myself with people I want to be like. There are only two kinds of people I want in my life. One of those people are those who give 110% in everything they do, because they believe they can do it. We can make the world a better place if we can work a little bit harder. The second kind of person I want in my life are those who are honest. I am honest with myself. I am honest in everything I do.

I once heard someone say that what you do in private is no one else's business. If I don't know what you are doing in the dark then how can I trust you? What you do in your life should be done whether you are alone or not. As a leader, you have to be 100% the same person who stands in front of people. Your story shouldn't have anything added or taken away. That is me and I am who I am. The people who know me know that I am just plain straightforward. Some people don't believe me when I tell them I don't have secrets.

If you want to be blessed, learn the life of Jesus Christ, and live humbly. I am becoming a Queen, and I already have my crown. I believe if we stopped watching TV, and put ourselves into the story of the successful, to understand the language of success we can be successful. With hard work, consistency, and positive thinking, and never quitting, no matter what the situation, we can achieve anything. Denzel Washington said when the devil leaves you alone that means you are in a group with them. If the devil is messing with you, that means you might be doing something right.

I truly believe that writing this book was a nightmare. I thought, I will never finish. All kinds of obstacles were coming my way, left and right. Yet, even though I was in hell, I still had a little light to shine. I don't need to switch any light or ask anybody for their light. I believed the light I needed to finish this book was within me. I prayed and I asked God what He wanted me to do. He said, whatever you want is on your fingertips. All He wanted for me was to finish this book and share my story. I cried a little bit, but I got up and made an agreement with God. I said, okay. Let me focus to finish this book and let me see what you can do within me.

Another thing I did was not keep quiet. When I heard the revelation from God, I shared it with Denise Nicholson. She was more excited for me than I was. Sometimes others will see your blessings before you. You can manifest the person you want to be. Believe me, I have experienced a lot of things in my thirty years, but I'll never take anything for granted. I am becoming me, and I believe all the wealth, all of the gold that people are looking for, is nowhere in this world. It is within us. We are the gold. We are the wealth. We are the happiness. We are the joy. We are the success. We are the powerful. We are the world changers. We are the people we are supposed to be.

We don't have to look elsewhere or point a finger to who the next Presidents will be, or who look to who is in the White House. We don't need to look at what Democrats or Republicans are doing. They have nothing to do with the light that God put in you. Use the little light that you have. Let it shine in your home. Shine In your community. Let it shine in your country. Let it shine into the world. JF Kennedy said,

"Don't ask what your country can do for you, ask what you can do for your country?" I think this question can be revised to say, don't ask what the world can do for you, ask what you can do to the world to make the world a better place to live in. Your footprint should influence your children. Your great-grandchildren should be Influenced by you for the rest of their lives. Simply because you are in the world, you should say: I am strong, I am smart, I am beautiful, I am marvelous, I am wonderfully made, I am the millionaire, I am a wealthy person. Say, I am that person who will leave something for the next generation.

You may ask, how can I know my calling? Consider when you see something and feel sad, and you wish you could do something about it. Think about when you see teenagers going to jail in America, and wish you could do something about it. All of these women and single mothers suffering. The struggle of refugees in America. You might see kids around-the-world, and wish you could do something. That thing is your calling. Your spirit is sent here through your body to accomplish greater things. That is why your spirit will never sleep.

God is a king and I know he has his Kingdom. He just wants us to accept his invitation for us to accomplish much in this world. I hope this book did not just wake you up or lead you to feel bad for me. I shared my story so that you can know that you can share yours. I wanted to be the voice of refugees, immigrants in America, or any western world. I want to let them know that it doesn't matter where they come from. They can make a difference in this world. It doesn't matter whether you have an education or not. My story may not touch your heart the way it does for others. Your story might not touch my heart the way it will touch other's hearts. A quote I really love says that if there is no enemy within, the enemy outside will do us no harm. This is an old African proverb. We all have the Spirit of Warriors within We have to stop thinking about escaping from the world. We belong here. When Jesus returns, we are only going to heaven for 1000 years, an old heaven and earth will pass away, and you will come to the new earth where you belong. You do not lose heaven, you lose earth. If we understood the principle that we are the only creatures who can make the world a better place, I believe we would find our ground. I believe we could help this world to be a better place for everyone to live in.

Even though you cannot help the whole world, you can make a difference in your little world. You can make your little world a better place for you to live in with your family and your community. Rejoice in your work! Thank you for reading my story. I truly believe that you are made for more and I can't wait to see what your little world will look like. I am creating mine, and I believe in myself. I am a beloved daughter of a king and I truly know who I am.

I am a Queen.

The Spirit of Warriors is within you!